FIT FOR A

Queen

Inside the Queen Mothers
Racing World

RICHARD PITMAN

This Edition First Published in 1995
by
Pride of Place (UK) Ltd
Specialist Sports Publishers

10 9 8 7 6 5 4 3 2 1

British Library Cataloguing in Publication Data.
A catalogue record for this book is available from
the British Library.

ISBN 1 874645 21 3

Printed by
BPC Wheatons Ltd

PRIDE OF PLACE (UK) LTD
UNIT 22, CBTC,
EUXTON LANE, CHORLEY
LANCASHIRE PR7 6TE

Also by Richard Pitman

Good Horses Make Good Jockeys
Guinness Guide to Steeplechasing
Steeplechasing
Martin Pipe; The Champion Trainer's Story

With Joe McNally

Warned Off
Hunted
Running Scared
Blood Ties (to be published October 1995)

To my mother Eve,
who is to me what the Queen Mother is to the Nation.
A person radiating kindness and overflowing with love,
leaving people all the better
for having come in contact with her.

Contents

Acknowledgments

My grateful thanks to those people who have contributed to this jaunt through 46 years of the Queen Mother's racehorse ownership, especially The Princess Royal and Michael Oswald C.V.O. Ivor Herbert's book, The Queen Mother's Horses, published by Pelham Books, Bill Curling's Royal Champion, published by Michael Joseph and Roger Mortimer's private account of the Life of Anthony Mildmay, proved to be an invaluable source of reference.

Foreword
by H.R.H. Princess Royal

BUCKINGHAM PALACE

The collection of pictorial memories and the stories behind them spans almost half of Queen Elizabeth The Queen Mother's lifetime and contains both the triumphs and disasters that make any branch of equestrian sport such a character building exercise. They also ensured that my Grandmother and I always had something to celebrate or commiserate about!

But it wasn't until I started to ride in races myself and then to own a National Hunt race horse that I really understood what had attracted and kept my Grandmother involved with National Hunt racing for so long. The places, the people and the horses have atmosphere, character, skill and bravery and, given the uncertainties and the huge potential for things to go wrong, there is also a degree of humility and real gratitude when things go right.

Owners come in all sorts, come rain or shine, from all walks of life, sharing a love of horses, and the Queen Mother is one of those owners without whom the sport might not exist. For the enjoyment of watching fit, well trained horses jumping fences at speed, the fear of a mistake, relief of a safe return or the sheer excitement of a close finish, has been, for my Grandmother, a life long pleasure.

Anne

Prelude

Her Majesty, Queen Elizabeth, The Queen Mother

"I've always wanted to have a horse for steeplechasing, of course The Queen is very keen on the flat. So I just thought I'd have one horse and see, it was no surprise when I got hooked, absolutely. I've had fun ever since.
It was Lord Mildmay actually who made me enthusiastic.
It's one of the real sports that's left to us isn't it? A bit of danger and a bit of excitement and those brave horses which is the best thing in the world. I've always loved them, ever since I was a little girl. The trouble is one gets too fond of them, I hate to see anything happen to them which I suppose is what every owner feels really.

Mr Cazalet was a good trainer, he was very strict. A great disciplinarian in the stables and with me too. One always loves to go and see the horses, the lads are very good, they get them really calm and it's a great experience. It's exciting, thrilling, seeing if the legs are all right and after evening stables are over I really enjoy that lovely sleepy stable time when the horses are eating.
The days spent at Fairlawne were great, they were lovely times. It could never be quite the same afterwards.
Mr Oswald looks after my racing interests and keeps an eye on everything, which is wonderful.
Raynham's marvellous for the young horses and those with strained legs. It's lovely and quiet there with beautiful paddocks. They are marvellously looked after, getting every attention and the legs seem to do well there, recovery comes which is great.

Major Wilson is splendid with the young horses. Oh he's a real character, I think he must have a touch of Irish in him.
Well of course, I read The Sporting Life. Get my day to day news, a little gossip which is always great fun. Oh yes, one likes to keep in touch.

Sandown Park is always a great favourite, with everybody I think. A wonderful course to see, it's always a thrill somehow.
It's a long job breeding National Hunt, very long term but it's worth it you know. It makes a big difference now so many fillies are running, it'll help the future to actually breed from those who have won races. It's all going on.
It was great gathering all the people who had ridden the horses for me, great fun. They all looked well and had survived which is a good thing.
I am so pleased to see my brilliant trainers... also the optimistic ones and the brave, brave jockeys. I'm now looking ahead to the 500th winner!
Steeplechasing is a real sporting thing still. I was thinking the other day, it must be 80% disappointment, or more perhaps. But that makes up when you do get a winner. I think it's well worth it. Oh, it is a great sport isn't it!"

1964

from
Elizabeth R

Fit For A Queen

Chapter 1

End of the Rainbow

Monday racing can often be mundane stuff yet the 30th May 1994 will remain burned into racegoers minds as it saw Nearco Bay add the modest sum of £2,749 to Queen Elizabeth's account but far more importantly, gaining her 400th winner over jumps.

The revamped course at Uttoxeter is a vibrant place these days due to the drive of former plumber turned spectacular businessman/entrepreneur, Stan Clarke. It was definitely the place to be on the eve of flaming June yet the one person who could have made the Staffordshire course and the tiny town explode into celebrations of nuclear proportions had to savour the moment via television.

The Queen Mother had a long standing luncheon date at Raymond Blanc's famous Oxfordshire hostelry, Le Manoir Aux Quat Saisons with, as luck would have it, a racing party. For the previous 9 years Queen Elizabeth had been entertained to a viewing of her young horses at Captain Charles Radclyffe's Lew House followed by an informal bite to eat and as a result of those happy, fun lunches which were cooked and presented by Monsieur Blanc, a visit was suggested to Le Manoir to explore the herb, vegetable and flower gardens there.

Michael Oswald, Queen Elizabeth's racing manager who also runs the Royal Studs at Sandringham, fills in the details. "The problem was to find a time of year when the gardens were at their best, the weather kind to us and when Queen Elizabeth could fit a visit into her very busy schedule. In order to match all these factors up, the date was fixed months in advance, but on the day coincided with the only possible

17

race left for Nearco Bay to attain the magical 400th success before the season ended five days later.

The decision came from Queen Elizabeth, both appointments would be met.

The day started with great excitement as Nearco Bay had won his last three races and was going to start favourite to make it four and in doing so get to the elusive landmark that not even the powerful battalions of the famous Dorothy Paget had managed.

Early morning telephone calls between us all and trainer Nicky Henderson, ascertained all was well with the chaser but that it would not be a pushover, Cheshire trainer Anne Hewitt's Bradwell had won a well contested chase just ten days earlier and had also beaten another of ours, Keep Talking, at Bangor on Dee in a thrilling finish a month before that.

We also had to respect Kim Bailey's fast ground specialist Far Senior, owned by Mrs Lois Duffy whose Mr Frisk won the 1990 Martell Grand National and Buddy Holly who received a stone in the handicap. All in all four of the five runners had good reasons for winning, it was never going to be easy and of course when a horse has set up a sequence of victories the pressure gets much more intense, not less. All winning runs come to an end but we all secretly prayed for 'just one more'.

If for whatever reason Nearco Bay failed to deliver this day, it meant we had to go right through until October when the horses were back from their summer rest, to try for the 400th winner."

So it transpired the horse, his trainer and Irishman John Kavanagh his rider, set off from Lambourn to Uttoxeter while Queen Elizabeth, Michael and his wife Lady Angela, who is a Lady in Waiting to The Queen Mother, headed to Le Manoir at Great Milton from London with Charles and Duse Radclyffe meeting the party there.

"It is such a really delightful place, the ambiance is perfect. It's not somewhere the likes of you and I could afford very often, if at all. It's nice to have seen it just once and the whole setting seemed exactly right for the momentous occasion it turned out to be.

Queen Elizabeth had declined the offer of a private room, opting to lunch in the public area," Michael Oswald recalled. "M. Blanc gave us a guided tour of the Manor and its incredible gardens then produced a

May 30th, 1994

The Queen Mother lunching at Le Manoir on the day Nearco Bay became her 400th winner. Monsieur Blanc shows the Royal party around his gardens.

meal fit for a Queen. Naturally the conversation featured the chances of Nearco Bay in the 3.30 pm, a three and a quarter mile chase with 22 fences to negotiate. We almost talked ourselves out of winning, there were so many things to thwart the important victory. Without doubt the calmest person amongst us was the owner who observed several times that as long as horse and rider came back safely, it would please her.

M. Blanc provided a small sitting room where we could watch the race on Channel Four. This meeting had not been in the scheduled coverage but Andrew Franklin recognised the importance of the occasion and took the decision to add the one race from Uttoxeter to his main coverage from Sandown Park that afternoon. We thought it was a brave and enterprising move, I was pleased for him as much as for ourselves that things went well. When we first heard what was planned, we thought it was fine but could all end in tears.

Nearco Bay is not the speediest of horses and so it turned out to be a pure slogging match all the way. Young John Kavanagh had a lot riding on his shoulders, more pressure than anyone else. He stuck to the task. Up with the pace from the very start, he actually got to the front at the 16th fence only to surrender the lead four jumps from home then fought his way back into the lead again two jumps from the finish and was all out to keep ahead of Bradwell who was every inch as honest as Nearco Bay.

You can imagine the atmosphere within the four walls of our room. Charles kept saying in his distinctive tone, 'I'm happy....yes I'm happy'. Queen Elizabeth and I replied every time, 'we're not ...we're not' and so it went on right to the line when we all erupted in quite a vocal fashion. It was just as well we were away from the public rooms as it would not have been possible to have been so demonstrative and believe me that is half the fun, letting pure emotion run riot.

Normally Queen Elizabeth treats both winning and losing exactly the same no matter what she is feeling inside. This was rather a unique occasion though!!

It would be difficult to imagine a more complete day, Queen Elizabeth was as happy for everyone involved as for herself, realising that a lot of people had contributed to this landmark from Norfolk to New Zealand. An added pleasure came from the fact that the racing public had always supported the Royal horses."

Nearco Bay was far from the first New Zealand horse to run in the Blue and Buff colours although he will be the one most people will remember because of this historic win. He had been sent over by his owner on an open ended lease. Marion Stevenson thought the chaser had done all he could do in his native country once he won The New Zealand Grand National, she wanted to see what he could do in Britain, the recognised pinnacle of the steeplechasing world so through Kim Clotworthy, who had been supplying New Zealand horses for many years, a deal emerged to suit all parties.

"He could be anything," Michael Oswald observes. "The key to him is the ground, he must have decent going. It is absolutely no use running him when the ground is soft or heavy. Given the right conditions he could win a Whitbread or even the elusive Grand National at Aintree. I would describe him as a fine big horse standing over 17 hands high. A clever jumper who is able to quickly find an extra leg after making a jumping error. Some horses take a while to organise themselves and recover from mistakes, Nearco Bay appears not to notice anything that from the grandstands stops our breathing for a moment or two.

His attributes are relentless galloping, unlimited stamina and total honesty. Was he the Tortoise or the hare?"

"Hare was not how I would have described him at first," trainer Nicky Henderson laughed. "He was the slowest horse in the stable and as I train 65 horses, it made me scratch my head somewhat. I mean, the winner of the New Zealand Grand National joins us with a huge reputation and is always struggling to keep up with even the moderate horses when we worked him at first. With young horses fancy pedigrees and correct conformation go straight out of the window once you start to gallop them at home but when one of proven ability can't go fast enough to keep himself warm, it is a worry. Being owned by the Queen Mother rather exaggerates that concern.

Most jumpers have periods of inactivity through strains and sprains, coughs and colds and over the past few years, virus. Nearco Bay arrived with a problem as he'd got a bit of a strained tendon before he flew over, then he knocked the other leg when messing about so he arrived with a question mark over both front legs.

Geoffrey Brain the renowned vet looked at his legs and decided the

21

best course of action was to inject them which I must say has worked wonders. He arrived in England in February 1992 and was unable to run that season. To recuperate he went up to Raynham, the beautiful Norfolk estate owned by Lord Townshend about fifteen miles from Sandringham where the young, the sick and the lame horses are cared for by Sylvia Palmer.

He spent the rest of that winter and the complete summer of 1993 in the parkland at Raynham before joining Mary Crouch's livery yard for his long steady hardening exercise doing road work. Mary lives nearby, only eight miles away from my Lambourn stables. You can imagine after eighteen months holiday it took a bit of work to turn the fat into muscle but on reflection that unplanned rest gave Nearco Bay the chance to acclimatise and may even have been a blessing in disguise.

John Kavanagh gets the response he needs from Nearco Bay at Uttoxeter. Aintree would hold no terrors for them?   (*Colin Turner*)

I told Michael Oswald several times the horse seemed slow but he did jump well and that quality wins races. It took me until January of 1994 to get him straight enough to flex his muscles on the racecourse at Windsor, almost two years from the day he arrived here.

Mick Fitzgerald rode him at a starting price of 25/1 which indicated there was little public support monetary wise although there was a great deal of interest generally. He led his eleven rivals for only two fences before faster horses took over then after a jumping mistake at the fourteenth, Mick sensibly pulled him up. We were encouraged.

Sadly when he reappeared three weeks later at Nottingham the petrol ran out before half way, he'd run worse than on his debut and we were all at a loss to explain why.

It was so embarrassing. I had little to report to either Michael or The Queen Mother and still the horse showed me nothing at home to suggest he'd ever win.

As the weather improved we decided to go back to nature by turning the gelding out in a paddock after exercise every day. He spent the daylight hours in the fresh air and although never in danger of setting the gallops alight, did work better.

Two things emerged, he appreciated the different routine and quite the opposite to what you would think of a slow horse, he liked the firmer ground. He was obviously sensitive to stable environment which through bedding and hay causes a certain amount of dust.

This learning process and recuperation period saw him absent from racecourse action for almost three months before we tried again at Hereford. Officially the going was soft but after one of my assistants walked the course we thought it would ride better than the official assessment and so it proved.

I'd chanced my luck a little even by entering in this race as it was confined to horses up to 100 and in our two previous races we were rated at 125. Luckily the handicapper took those races on face value and let us in which gave us a chance of competing at a lower level.

Nearco Bay started at 10/1 with few people wanting to back him even at those odds. He won nicely under John Kavanagh who came in for the ride as Mick Fitzgerald was riding elsewhere. John is a quiet almost shy person whose has an infinity with horses and can get the best out of them.

It was the Queen Mother herself who said it would be the correct thing to do to keep John on the horse as they had struck up a winning partnership. If at any stage he is unable to partner Nearco Bay then naturally Mick Fitzgerald will return to his saddle.

We went back to Hereford on 30th April where we won again, this time as 6/4 favourite, then made it a hat trick of victories over course and distance in mid-May. Would you believe it, the slowest horse in the stable actually broke the track record that day . It had stood for ten years. There has to be a moral to this story but I'm blowed if I can think of one.

When it came to the last attempt I had a choice of Uttoxeter and Wetherby, eventually deciding on the former. I get very wound up at the races but this time I was awful. Poor Diana, my wife, must have wondered if it was the same man she'd married. If the situation had not been bad enough as it was, to have this weighty occasion televised heightened the load.

It came about the week before when at a dinner Channel 4 Boss Andrew Franklin asked if anything exciting was in the offing. Stupidly I told him of our aim which was like telling a man dying of thirst in the desert where the well was situated. Andrew wasted no time in adding the Uttoxeter chase into his programme from Sandown.

We all could have done without the eyes of the world on us that day. I thought how stupid I'd been to add to our burden yet all worked out for the best.

Even the course commentator, Johnny Turner, added to the agony by announcing as they galloped to the first fence 'The nations best wishes go out to her Majesty.' Now that is almost as tempting to fate as saying 'He's only got to jump the last to win!!!'

Nearco Bay's victory meant our stable had provided Queen Elizabeth with her last five winners as Whitechapel had also done his bit. It occurred to me on the drive home, exhausted from worry and post race relief, that we'd done the easy bit. Just imagine all the heartache and glory that had gone before us to get the owner the previous 395 successes.

I did not phone Queen Elizabeth from the car as mobiles are not secure enough but as soon as we got home contact was made. Naturally the moment was euphoric with the elated owner refusing to take any credit, she kept saying 'Oh you are so clever'.

But I know that what we'd done was the same as we do for any horse here, worked hard to find the key which in his case was nothing more than fresh air, Mother Nature and fast going."

It had been almost two years to the day since Nicky got the call from Michael Oswald to invite him to become one of the Royal trainers, the very day he and Diana moved into historic Seven Barrows stables. Moving in such lofty circles was not strange to the Hendersons as his father Johnny was for many years a trustee of Ascot racecourse and is now Lord Lieutenant of Berkshire. Even so it is every trainer's dream to handle the Royal horses.

At Nicky Henderson's Seven Barrows Stables in November 1994. The day the front cover photographs were taken. (l to r; Michael Oswald, The Queen Mother's Racing Manager, Diane Henderson, The Queen Mother and Lady Angela Oswald) (*Bernard Parkin*)

Last November Queen Elizabeth visited the stables for the third successive year to watch her horses school on Nicky's enviable private facilities. This time the occasion was also used to obtain a photo to be used for the Royal Christmas card 1994. A unique year!

The theme running throughout this book is the kindness and fun loving nature Queen Elizabeth possesses. She enjoys the company of the characters that the uncertainty of jump racing attracts. Nicky Henderson recalls, "Queen Elizabeth was attending a luncheon at The Savoy where I had the pleasure of sitting next to her. We had a runner in the 3.10 pm race at Fontwell Park that day and she quietly ventured, 'Do you think we will be able to slip away in time to watch the horse? If you can follow me'."

Nicky had visions of the party trooping into the local Ladbrokes betting shop but not a bit of it, "We managed to make an exit a 2.55pm. I'd lined up a taxi well in advance in case we made it and when I jumped in and told the cabby 'Follow that car' he thought he landed a part in a film. After a few streets he twigged we were chasing the Royal Rolls Royce and questioned my motives. Well, we cornered around Eros' statue, hurtled through the Clarence House gates inches behind The Queen Mother in what must have looked like an emergency to the tourists. We rushed into the house and up the stairs just in time to watch the race on SIS, the Satellite System that televises up to five race meetings a day. I only hope that I can move as smartly when I reach the age of 94."

Other Royal homes including Buckingham Palace take the system which is available to public subscription, displaying the value mother and daughter put on their horseracing.

"Another incident that shows how much regard Queen Elizabeth holds for steeplechasing came after Nearco Bay's second win at Hereford. This meeting was not covered by SIS but as I had obtained a copy from the racecourse and was going to Heathrow that evening it was suggested a slight detour would enable the proud owner to see the victory that same day.

Queen Elizabeth was in residence at The Royal Lodge, her Windsor home in the middle of the park and although I'd been there before, it is far from easy to find. After driving around in vain for a while with my flight time getting even closer, I spotted a Range Rover and gave chase flashing my lights and using the horn to stop the vehicle to obtain directions. The driver refused to accede to my desperate efforts and continued to accelerate until forced to stop for some riders. I jumped out, ran up to the car and thumped on the window for attention. Imagine my horror as the window revealed Prince Philip as the driver - Have you ever wished the ground would open?

He was most helpful, set me on the right path and not only was Queen Elizabeth able to see that days winner on tape, I got my plane."

Travelling head lad John Worrall, jockey John Kavanagh and lad Glyn Foster after Nearco Bay won at Uttoxeter and became the Queen Mother's 400th winner. *(Bernard Parkin)*

Author, Richard Pitman meets the Queen Mother after winning the Welsh Champion Hurdle on Lanzarote in 1975. His admiration for her has grown in the twenty years since.

For jockey John Kavanagh being associated with the historic milestone is something that will remain alive with him for ever.

The 26 year old from Cullihill in Co. Laois is one of ten children and of his six brothers; not one of them would ride at thirteen stones nor do they have any interest in doing so. He knows Nearco Bay inside out and treats him like any other horse. Having no horsy background there was no easy way in but horses had always fascinated him. While his chums knocked seven bells out of each other on the hurling pitch, John opted to spend his pocket money on riding lessons then swapped work in the stables for free tuition.

He left home at fourteen eventually ending up with Henderson of whom he says, "We've been lucky and we totally understand each other. I'm not the most stylish jockey but horses settle and jump well for me. I feel I quickly get to understand each new horse.

Nearco Bay has got some speed in a race but it only lasts for two furlongs. I like to switch him off for a while, let him jump out of my hands without asking too much then creep to the leaders and pounce two fences from the finish. If the ground is good or better still, fast, I would give up the rest of my riding career to partner this chap in the Grand National. He has everything needed to put right the tragic result of the 1956 race when the Queen Mother's Devon Loch collapsed twenty yards from the finish with the race won."

Chapter 2

The New Zealand Connection: Kim Clotworthy

Nearco Bay came to race here after New Zealand trainer and horse dealer, Kim Clotworthy had reported back to Michael Oswald that he had seen the horse that would crown the Queen Mother's already incredible involvement in jumping.

He first noted the big bay gelding only three days after being let out of hospital where he'd been in traction for six weeks to pull his broken neck back into line. This action is typical of the tough, wiry horseman whose grandfather had emigrated from Ireland a hundred years ago.

Kim's son Shaun was playing in the Rugby Championships in the South Island at Dunedin, ten hours car journey, no deterrent despite his weakened state after so long immobile. They stopped off to check over some horses on the way, watched Shaun's team take the honours on the rugby field and had a "Hell of a party afterwards" where Kim met some fellow North Islanders who took him off the next day to caste his eye over Nearco Bay and another horse called Rainman owned by Marion and Drew Stevenson.

Rainman was bought but the big bay could not be prized away from his devoted owners. Kim watched the horses progress as he took maiden, then novice races, even winning two days in succession. The horse had more potential than Kim had seen for many years, the snag was that his owners thought so too and wanted to realise that rare commodity themselves.

In June of 1991 Kim attended Royal Ascot where he received a luncheon invitation in the Royal Box. Queen Elizabeth quickly cast a fly in her guest's direction as she is so expert at doing when fishing for salmon, saying, "Now then Kim, I have heard there is another good horse but his lady owner does not want to sell him? I think she will prove too strong for you, you will not win this one."

"She teased me although I did not need any goading, I wanted this one more than any I'd bought before. I'd told Michael Oswald that an offer of $45,000 (equivalent to £15000) had been turned down, prompting him to instruct me to go to double that, which back home was unheard of yet in Ireland was a fraction of the sums similar horses fetched. I left for home as confident of getting Nearco Bay as I've ever been in my life of anything and before we ever talked of a price Marion Stevenson told me if ever he came on the market, he'd be mine. This at least proved some consolation as there were some Americans with large cheque books floating around buying horses to go jumping.

Marion wanted to win The New Zealand Grand National run in August, which he duly did but I never went near her at the races as the victory plus the celebrations were hers.

At the evening party she asked me to sit on a tree stump and talk but when she burst into tears it knocked me out of my stride. I was prepared for anything except that situation and as a result of the dramatic situation we never even mentioned a deal.

The same evening in the Hotel I had to witness the Aussies whip us at rugby, it could not have been a worse time.

My final request to her as we all set off for our homes was done by letter, the likes of which I've never managed before or since, it was a good letter, my best shot. I said in it that I would phone her for an answer the next week and as I'd been given a deadline by Michael Oswald, if we were to get the horse over for the current season, it was now or never.

When I reached Marion Stevenson on the phone she paused for what seemed for ever then said she would not sell the horse. Just as I was about to strangle myself with the telephone cable in despair she ventured that she would lease him to Queen Elizabeth for a year.

Michael Oswald came as close to swearing, as I've ever known him to come, at the news. The home breds were not promising and most

'The Homestead'

Kim Clotworthy prepares another young horse for daily exercise.

of the others were injured or patched up, he needed a sound horse to fly the flag and this was it. The plan we hatched was to run him straight off the plane, before he had time to feel the enormous change in time and diet which would make him go off the boil for a few months.

When the horse came to me for the journey, he had slight signs of a tendon injury so we shelved the plan until March of 1992. We stopped overnight at Frankfurt where the stable had a high door with a small gap above it for ventilation, and for some reason, Nearco Bay took exception to being closed in and ended up getting both front legs over the top of the door. It meant that when we arrived, I presented Nicky Henderson with a horse standing on only two sound legs, the whole thing had gone horribly wrong.

The original lease ran for a year, we got an extension then to end in April of this year (1995) and I'm sure in view of what Nearco Bay is doing now, that will run on indefinitely. Marion Stevenson is a sports-woman and thrilled to think the horse may attempt to win the Whitbread or even to lay Devon Loch's ghost."

The New Zealand Grand National is run at Riccarton, Christchurch on the South Island. It is a tough race with bigger, stiffer brush fences than any in Britain, the most famous jump being Cutts's Brush, standing 5'3" high and so wide and solid that a mini car is often driven along the top to illustrate the nature of the obstacle.

Kim Clotworthy weighs up his life among horses with the disarming honesty and character that typifies the people who have been drawn to Queen Elizabeth throughout her racing involvement. He knows why racing folk are sounder than in some other walks of life. "In racing you will meet the best and the worst people, all you have to do is sort one from the other. Those who can't take a beating well, disappear sooner rather than later," are his observations.

"My mother, Peg, was a great Royalist. She read and saved every-thing printed about the family, she even took me aged six, on a 5 hour trek over dirt tracks to catch a glimpse of Queen Elizabeth when she visited Auckland in 1948.

As I remember I was not too excited at being dragged all over the country to catch a brief glimpse of a hat on the head of someone I could not relate to. My mother would have been so proud to think that forty years later her son and his family would be invited to Clarence

House and Buckingham Palace for tea. I've had a great buzz out of life and it's not finished yet."

Picking Nearco Bay did not constitute a lucky selection. The previous four horses he'd sent over had each proved a shrewd buy and all seemed to attract more than the usual share of adventures en route.

In 1981 Sindebele set the ball rolling as a five year old and having won several flat races, he was the sort to get straight on with, trained by the new Royal handler, Fulke Walwyn. When Fulke was told the gelding had been bought in New Zealand, he was asked if he had ever been there? "No", came the gruff reply. Would he like to go out to see the horse? "Not bloody likely", was the even gruffer response.

So it was left to the man who had bought the horse to fly over with him. To this day Kim is convinced disaster would have ensued if he had not done so and that is no idle boast. Let him pick the story up.

"There were 110 horses of all descriptions on the plane as well as some sheep and several llama on board. The flight became a nightmare with animals fighting and more than once horses were galloping loose around the plane.

Worse still, a fire developed in one engine and we had to be diverted to Manchester as their fire fighting equipment was far superior to where we were scheduled to land. Few of the other horse handlers knew of the problem but as I'd been up in the cockpit when the request was put over for firefighters to be alerted, I had information I'd preferred not to have been in possession of.

As we touched down, a stream of fire engines raced alongside us spraying foam over the plane until we came to a halt. Once safely off the plane, the facilities for such a large amount of animals were almost non existent and I refused to accept where they wanted to put Sindebele. They said his quarantine had not been completed but I knew different.

I caused such a fuss that a horsebox was summoned only to prove totally inadequate for a racehorse and especially one destined to race for the Queen Mother. The floorboards were almost worn through in places and nails protruded from the ancient struts.

Having brought the horse half way around the world and managed to protect it from the mayhem on the journey, I was damned if I was going to let him deteriorate at this stage of my mission. I phoned Fulke Walwyn, told him where we were and asked for a lorry to be sent up to collect us and within four and a half hours we were heading for

Lambourn in defiance of the shouts and threats of the vet who wanted us to Quarantine where any decent animal lover would not keep pigs.

It had been 50 hours since we'd taken off back home, 55 when we finally walked into Fulke's old fashioned stables bedded with the most golden straw I'd ever seen.

Sindebele did win at Cheltenham then sadly he had to be put down after falling two hurdles from home, having just taken the lead. There is no doubt this could have been a very useful racehorse had he lived.

I'd flown over specifically to see him run, it turned out to be a terrible day for everyone.

Sindebele (NZ) winning at Cheltenham (S. Shilston) in 1982. This could have been a champion had he lived. The first New Zealand bred horse sent over by Kim Clotworthy. *(Bernard Parkin)*

Any true horseman is sad when hearing of a horse 'Tapping the mat' (dying). My brief had been to find a horse to win races, one that would not cost a lot of money, not because the intended owner had a limited purse but it would not have presented the right face to buy success. Sindebele was bought for a fraction of the cost of a similar horse in Europe.

My first impressions of the trainer were not over endearing until he admitted that the horse looked in superb condition. You see, no matter how upset or whatever his thoughts of this rough little newcomer bringing a breed of horse he'd no experience of, Fulke was a master horseman and he recognised the amount of care it had taken to make such a journey and still look like a racehorse.

I rode out the very next morning but the lads were not friendly, they thought of me as just another privileged visitor taking all the best rides without having earned them. When I asked for and got to ride the worst behaved mounts and showed the boys I could do so, their attitudes changed and acceptance followed. I've had many a good night in the Malt Shovel pub adjacent to the yard.

As Sindebele had shown every sign of being good, the message came for me to replace him and although I had slight misgivings, it was decided to chance a big black handsome horse I'd got called Matuba Matuba, named after a famous African chief who'd reputedly fathered six hundred children from a string of wives.

Michael Oswald was keen to have him while insisting the name be changed as the history did not fit. The British racing press would want to know the background.

This time the journey over went without a hitch and again I was asked up to the Royal Box at Sandown Park to meet the Queen Mother. No sooner had we met than she opened up her handbag to produce photographs of her new horse and said, 'We renamed him Harbour Master, I do think it is a shame we changed it though'."

Harbour Master finished second three times then contracted a virus and died. Even so, despite both New Zealand horses meeting premature endings, the source looked right enough.

The next southern hemisphere horse to race for the Queen Mother came after a prompt from the former Epsom supremo Tim Neligan, who was down under attending an international conference on racing. He had been primed by Michael Oswald to stir Kim Clotworthy into action. Aware of the importance of his brief, Kim had been steady in his actions and although mentioned as a suitable replacement, had not attempted to make it the next Royal purchase.

The horse in question was The Argonaut, who at that time was doing a stint of three day eventing aged four. He'd been bought by Cydne Evans who, like Kim, was attracted to the gelding at the yearling sales. She got the better of the auction but the determined Royal horse spotter had kept tabs on the horse under Cydne's tutorledge and knew that one day he'd get him for the job he'd been bred for.

Further fuelled by Neligan's enthusiasm when he got back to

England, Michael Oswald upped the pressure for the gelding to be bought. On the final occasion he phoned, Michael had forgotten the time difference and when he got through it was one o'clock in the morning, three and a half hours after Kim normally went to bed being an early riser.

Covered yards where most horses are kept overnight at Kim Clotworthy's home. Horses are turned out in the paddocks during the day, due to the good climate.

However, on this occasion a party was still going strong and as the whiskey had drained Kim's resolve, he sent Karen his wife to take the call. When it transpired it was business, Kim made the effort to take in Michael's request to stop messing about and finalise the deal. "I think I got the colour and sex of the horse right but must have sounded pretty vague regarding the relevant details and there is no doubt Michael knew I'd had a skinful.

Cydne did not part easily with the horse that she had schooled on from the yearling stage but we got him and as Mark Todd was flying over to the Los Angeles Olympics with Charisma, I entrusted him with the newest Royal charge. He is by the stallion Showoff and lived up to that horse's name. A big handsome brown horse, he did the Queen Mother proud winning 15 races in her colours."

Dalliston became the fourth horse Kim supplied only this time he and Michael hatched a plot to prepare the horse in New Zealand and run him soon after he touched down in England. The brown gelding had been bought by Kim as a yearling to win The Derby two years later and although placed on the flat, had looked more of a potential jumper.

To bring him to peak prior to his flight to England, it was agreed to give Dalliston an outing in a 'schooling trial', which he won by 10 lengths. Upgraded to running against other trials winners in an open trial, he did the same again with ease.

Michael Oswald gave the nod to a run in Queen Elizabeth's colours, when plagued by bad luck in running he only finished fourth of the eighteen starters. The colours were flown out especially by Air New Zealand and the event caused a great deal of interest

The racecaller gave the horse a great build up, the orders were to come late in the race to win. Dalliston flew all right but when he finally got out of the bunch, it was too late to catch the first three. He had not been able to give the enthusiastic crowd the result they'd hoped for, yet he'd not disgraced himself either.

Nevertheless the plot had been well primed and the long journey got underway. The 1200 mile hop to Australia went without a hitch then the whole thing ground to a halt as their plane was required to service the Gulf War which had just erupted.

A promise of two days' delay crept up to four, alerting Kim that if he was to maintain fitness, he'd have to get some work into the horse while waiting.

Kim laughs at the lengths he went to as the horse was still under quarantine restrictions and was being checked daily at 9 a.m. by a gruff ministry vet of Irish extraction. "At first thinking it would only be for a day or two, I cantered around the lawn at the stables. The hoof-prints caused some concern so I looked for other grass and found it a few hundred yards away in the Centennial Park in the middle of Sydney.

Word got about and the ministry man tried hard to catch me breaking quarantine restrictions which would have impounded the horses and scuppered the training schedule. Several times when he checked on me the horse had been hosed off and he naturally refused to believe I'd done it to stop him sweating.

By then we'd been grounded for 16 days and as the ministry man warned me he knew what I was doing, I kept to the quarantine yard for two days.

It coincided with Christmas and as my father had a terminal illness I flew back home on Christmas morning, watched the New Zealand Derby on Boxing Day then rejoined Dalliston who'd been well cared for by a girl groom I trusted to stick by his side.

I decided to come clean with Michael and told him that I would have to risk finding another work place but would need to do it in the middle of the night to avoid detection. If I landed in the soup I needed him to back me. I think he quite liked the intrigue. In his position things had to be done correctly but I think this little hide and seek game excited him a bit.

Not far from the quarantine enclosure in the heart of residential Sydney there is a communal park of about twenty acres with rugby and other games pitches on it. The perimeter was fenced by post and rails and the entrance gates locked at night. To get to it we needed to cross a six lane highway which meant venturing out when things were quietest.

Sydney's like any other major city in the world is alive late into the night and busy long before dawn with deliveries and early shift workers. I decided the best time to safely cross the highway and be seen by as few people as possible would be just after 2 a.m. Dalliston and I would have to jump into the park over the railings so I did a recce of the perimeter to find a decent spot under a streetlamp to give him a clear view of the jump in and, if we stayed together, out again!!

The place I chose was opposite a high-rise block of flats. Imagine the little drama unfolding outside their windows as the occupiers slept?

We popped the railings without a hitch, did a good exercise around the rugby pitches and jumped back out all within the space of ten minutes without seeing another soul. Obviously a trail of hoofprints would alert the park keepers but I reasoned they would not figure out how, let alone why, they were there. I decided to risk it one more night having been assured the plane would be leaving two days later.

It went well the second night too, even though Dalliston got a bit cocky jumping the railings in the false light, taking them on faster than I'd planned. On the second circuit of the pitches, lights in some of the flats winked on and as a bewildered audience wiped the sleep out of their eyes, we flew back over the railings and disappeared into the night.

They must have sworn to their workmates they'd seen the ghost of Phar Lap, then taken the Doubting Thomas's into the park to see the hoofprints.

The ministry man would barely grunt at me at that time and although he dearly would have liked to refuse my exit papers, he had no positive proof I'd broken Quarantine. When I had the horse loaded up I thanked him for his help then told him what I thought of his unhelpful ways ending with the barb, 'You know the difference between us, don't you? My ancestors were immigrants, yours were prisoners!!' While he fumed after me, I ran up the ramp and only hope I'm not under his jurisdiction again."

Kim Clotworthy is a hard working, fun loving character. He is straight and true, knows his job better than most. He trained Uncle Remus to win The New Zealand Derby in a run of eleven consecutive victories. He is equally at ease chatting to the Queen Mother as he is drinking a pint with the lads.

Chapter 3

Lord Mildmay:
The Instigator of the Royal
Hobby

How proud Lord Mildmay would have been had he lived to witness the way Queen Elizabeth's steeplechasing interests have flourished, as it was he who first suggested that she have a horse in training with his long time friend Peter Cazalet.

Only one short year after the incredible story fluttered into operation in 1949 with the acquisition of Monaveen shared with her daughter, then Princess Elizabeth, Anthony Mildmay failed to return from an early morning swim from his private beach at Mothecombe, a few miles east of Plymouth. His body never surfaced and to this day his nephew Anthony Mildmay-White, who chairs the Disciplinary Committee of The Jockey Club, is convinced the cause was directly due to cramp and the effect of old neck injuries.

Lord Mildmay had endured a particularly tiring week and on his way to the sea before breakfast on May 12th 1950 he called into his stables to let his groom know he would not be riding that morning. He made a habit of taking a basin to wash the sand from his feet before slipping into his shoes for the return uphill walk through the gardens of

Mothecombe House and when he failed to return, only the filled basin on the edge of the sand flagged Lord Mildmay's final movements.

Only two days before his death the champion amateur jockey had lost a race at Ludlow when gripped by cramp in his neck. It seems the cold sea water brought on an attack and the people's favourite became powerless to fight the might of the English Channel.

The official search went on for days on end and when it became apparent that Lord Mildmay had not been swept into one of the numerous rocky bays around that part of the coast, the inevitable was accepted. Even knowing a miracle was needed to change the result, the staff of The Flete Estate continued their own lonely watch around the rugged shore for a further three weeks.

At that time Anthony Mildmay had a tremendous following among the racegoing public who appreciated his prowess in the saddle and sensed his ease with those who had not been fortunate enough to be born into the same privileged world as he.

The loss of such a man in those circumstances reverberated around the corridors of power and in racing orientated pubs alike. Memorial services were held simultaneously in London, at Shoreham and also at his home. Lord Mildmay was laid to rest at Mothecombe where he died, with just his sister Helen, her husband John and his long time friend and adventure sharer Peter Cazalet to wave farewell, aged forty one.

Peter Cazalet survived his friend by twenty three years and it could not have been more fitting that his name should be added to The Mildmay Memorial Chase at Sandown Park to become The Cazalet, Mildmay Memorial. These two sportsmen would have wished to be coupled in racing's memory as a team rather than as individuals.

To commemorate the great man, there is The Mildmay of Flete competed for at the Cheltenham Festival every March and also the Park Course at Aintree is called The Mildmay Course.

With large houses in Shoreham, near Sevenoaks in Kent, London, Berkeley Square and the Flete Estates in which to develop as a child, Anthony Mildmay forged links that stayed strong throughout his short life.

Although at Eton at the same time as Cazalet, Lord Mildmay had little contact, as expected when two years age separated them and, to compact the divide, Cazalet excelled at sport whereas Mildmay did not.

Cambridge saw the start of his racing interests which became so passionate that it lured Queen Elizabeth into the sport. My, how both she and it gained by the involvement. Anthony Mildmay rode in numerous point to points at Cottenham while at Cambridge without ever experiencing that surge of adrenaline a winner provides. He did get off the mark though, at the Dartmoor point to point on a horse belonging to his father, little realising the influence he would have on generations to come.

Conversely, Peter Cazalet had enjoyed considerable success in the saddle during his time at Oxford, having shown a total disregard for horses before that time of his life.

The friendship became cemented in the pair's early days of work, Cazalet's home, Fairlawne, being close to Mildmay's at Shoreham. Even though Mildmay was the lesser in everything they'd done during their teens, no divide was evident and, indeed, Peter Cazalet gave his neighbour a chaser of his own after the first meeting at Fairlawne. The fact it died of a heart attack only two weeks later did nothing to dampen the blossoming union.

Helped though not encouraged by his father, Anthony Mildmay learned from experience when buying cheap young horses from Ireland to put into training at Fairlawne and both he and his new-found friend flourished. Neither ever became jealous of the other's victories, which is a real test of character and in this case, it never altered.

Being six feet two inches tall yet weighing only ten stones, strength in the saddle could never be accredited to Anthony Mildmay and often he suffered the indignity of parting company with his mounts in the first few years of raceriding.

Outweighing this weakness, Anthony Mildmay possessed a determined spirit to succeed and also had no sense of fear. These attributes carried him far in a game where there is no room for doubts.

His first winner under National Hunt Rules came at the now defunct Wye racecourse in Kent in his very first season and only a month later, he rode Youtell in The Grand National. The unexpected often happens in this greatest of all steeplechases and this venture did not stray from the script, they fell at the first fence breaking the rider's nose.

Anthony visited the winner's enclosure several times before the season ended but few gave him more satisfaction than when winning on the grey Yarmouth at another defunct course, Buckfastleigh, the nearest track to his Devon home. The final score reached five wins in his first season, with Peter Cazalet still managing to better his friend by one winner.

The bond firmed even further when Anthony joined Peter and his wife Leonora for dinner at The Grange and was asked to stay the night. He never returned to live at his own home again, even when the Cazalets moved into the main house at Fairlawne.

That unusual relationship later survived a radical change in the household when sixteen years later, following Leonora's surprise and premature death in 1944 after a minor operation, Peter Cazalet married his second wife Zara. He had warned his close friend that it would be doubtful that he could continue the arrangement, yet Zara Cazalet warmed to the man who had become part of the furniture and extended her welcome to leave things as they were.

Zara Cazalet, now past her mid seventies, is still a strikingly beautiful woman with the zest and exuberance of a person in their thirties. Although a London dweller her country visits are numerous and extensive, visiting her children and continuing the link with Queen Elizabeth forged almost fifty years ago.

"Queen Elizabeth had been to see us quite a few times once the bond had been established through having Monaveen trained at Fairlawne, then King George came down to luncheon shortly before he died. Peter and I agreed the purpose of his visit was to establish in his own mind that we were all right, that we were fit for a Queen." Zara Cazalet casts her mind back. "Peter had thought that when he retired as a public trainer he'd continue to have a smaller string of his own and Queen Elizabeth's. It was not to be.

For twenty years Queen Elizabeth came to stay at Fairlawne in December and over the past twenty two years since I have been widowed I have been a regular houseguest of Queen Elizabeth's, including at her Scottish retreat at Birkhall. She is the kindest and most considerate friend. Only a few years ago when travelling to Birkhall to stay, I crashed my B.M.W. estate, it was a write off but neither myself nor my little Pekinese were hurt other than being quite shocked. At the time I did not have a mobile phone and it seemed ages before the police came along to rescue me. They kindly contacted Birkhall to let them know what had happened and that I would be late arriving for dinner.

A police van took me there and he assumed I was a maid, especially

The Queen Mother at Fairlawne, where the majority of her incredible total of winners were trained.

when I told him to take me around to the back entrance. As it was 9.15 p.m. by then I assumed everyone would be half way through dinner and did not want to interrupt them. However, as we swung in front of the house the whole place was lit up with Queen Elizabeth's private secretary Sir Alistair Aird at the door, the place awash with floodlights and there right behind Alistair stood Queen Elizabeth. So thoughtful and caring and what's more she insisted the driver went in to have something to eat and warming to drink.

I curtsied and kissed her, she was so worried for me and while walking me to my room Queen Elizabeth pressed three little homeopathic pills into my hand and said 'You must be somewhat shocked, take these now, they will relieve any anxiety and settle you down.'

Both she and I are ardent supporters of homeopathic remedies and have been for most of our lives. Another occasion when I arrived at Birkhall to stay Queen Elizabeth said 'Don't kiss me, I've got this silly little chesty complaint,' to which I asked had she seen a doctor, 'No, of course not, I cured the fever with a course of homeopathic pills.' Silly of me to even have asked if she'd seen a doctor, she's a tough Scottish lassie, that's the answer to it. We both believe in healers too.

Three years ago when Queen Elizabeth was the illest she has ever been due to persistent bronchial trouble, I must say I was then very worried about her, she went to a reflexologist in Norfolk who cures every kind of ailment by manipulation of the toes. It worked too !

The alternative medicine train of thought also extends to animals. My late husband Peter, the Royal Studs and the current trainers often use Radionics known as 'The Box'. My former sister in law, Lavinia Duchess of Norfolk, put Peter on to it while Lady Murless alerted Michael Oswald to the benefits. We don't pretend to understand how it works but have seen remarkable results."

Basically the analysis is done when a lock of the horse's or for that matter, human's hair is sent to the operator. The hair acts as a link between the patient and the radionic equipment which scans the functions of all the patient's systems, measuring and recording malfunctions, infections, injuries or blockages.

Having established what is wrong, the treatment is projected from a variety of instruments specially designed for the purpose of curing the ailment. The most amazing aspect is that the patient is treated wherever they are in the world as effectively as if they were in the same room as the equipment. Animals respond well to radionic treatment, producing a higher success ratio due to the fact that they have a definite will to get better. Allergies can be eliminated, fractures knitted more quickly, wounds healed and infections cleared up. The diagnosis also will pinpoint troubles that require manipulation or physiotherapy.

Countless successful cases can be quoted and indeed I saw the before and after effects of using 'The Box' on The Queen's mare Soprano. The mare had continued to lose condition despite eating well, she looked a shell of her former self and there was grave concern for her life. I took some hairs from her mane to Mrs Lavender Dower, near Burford in Gloucestershire, for analysis and treatment and two months later saw the results myself, total recovery without patient ever meeting the healer.

This alternative to vetenary medicine is still being used as it was when Anthony Mildmay gained another five winners in his second season in 1933/34. His intended Grand National partner proved inadequate to even get to Aintree, a goal which appeared to be both trainer and rider's burning ambition.

A solitary success in his third season from 44 rides was bolstered by a second ride in The National on a miserable horses called Master Orange who downed tools on the second circuit and refused. The next day Anthony rode Irish Flight in the Foxhunter's Chase, which in 1935 was still being run over the full National course and distance.

The trip made no difference as Irish Flight buried his rider at the first breaking his arm and some ribs, injured a lung, bruised internal workings and badly concussed him. In fact, as he was stretchered off the course a priest took the precaution of administering the last rites.

Four short months later the bold amateur started the new season at the first meeting, the jumping crowd accorded him with a hero's reception when he equalled his last year's score in a single, satisfying day. Things progressed well with 14 winners in the bag before the ten month season drew to a close.

That year Anthony pursued his Aintree dream further when selecting Davy Jones to buy for the Grand National. The sum of £650 his father paid was a big price for a tubed horse who had just won his novice chase at Gatwick. What's more the 17 hands high chestnut was still an entire. Another Gatwick win, followed by a gallant second at Manchester, promised the lanky amateur the best chance he'd ever had at Aintree.

History within racing circles seems to keep throwing up names linked through decades and the 1936 National proved the point. Peter Cazalet rode his own Emancipator and Fulke Walwyn partnered the former National winner Reynoldstown. No one could have guessed that both men would have the honour and pleasure of guiding the bulk of The Queen Mother's steeplechasers to today's historic number of wins and indeed, it would be another thirteen years to Monaveen's embryonic start.

Davy Jones and the sporting Anthony Mildmay lined up at odds of 100/1 for the National, yet ten minutes later those odds looked likely to let the bookies off the hook, although the second favourite Golden Miller had already ensured them of a bumper pay day by getting no further than the first fence. Davy Jones led the field a merry gallop and was still in front of the eighteen left standing when going out into the country for the second circuit.

Anthony Mildmay on Davy Jones leads the field in the 1936 Grand National with his friend and trainer Peter Cazalet in 4th place.

Avenger, the favourite, fell at the next and by Becher's Brook only Fulke Walwyn and Reynoldstown had any chance of posing a challenge. Davy Jones snatched at the second last fence causing Anthony to sit back in the saddle letting the reins slip through his fingers allowing the horse enough freedom to find a leg to recover from the mistake.

Nightmare! When his hands got to the buckle end of the reins, the metal pin slipped out and where there should have been a firm grip prior to gathering up the reins for an assault on the final fence, there was nothing. With no steering nor brakes Davy Jones took the easy way out by running around the final jump through the big crowd, oblivious to his rider's desperate attempt to guide him with his whip.

One second another Grand National fairy story looked on the cards, the next fate played a cruel hand as Reynoldstown swept to victory under a jubilant Walwyn. Peter Cazalet's last sighting of his less fancied runner as his own mount cried enough four fences from home, was of his best friend and the horse he trained for Anthony Mildmay, sweeping to victory. Can you imagine the stomach blow when trotting back past the grandstands he heard the result with no mention of Davy Jones in the first three places?

If enough of the future had not been already spotted in this race, who would have laid 100/1 that exactly twenty years later a similar, though worse fate would befall another Cazalet trained runner in the very same race? Devon Loch trumped the happening of 1936 to continue the mystique of this emotional event. Peter Cazalet's strength of character saw him take this knock fair and square on the chin as he did with everything else in life be it triumph or disaster.

British sports followers love a gallant loser almost more than an easy winner, so Anthony Mildmay became a celebrity overnight without ever being effected himself by the public's affection. Courage combined with cruel ill-fortune has always been a British recipe for the public to take a person into their hearts, regular success sometimes having the opposite effect. Another 14 winners had been added to the total by then.

Having set up a Nursery under an acre of glass at Shoreham, Anthony found the way to ease his journeys between the market garden and his family home in Devon was to use his small plane which he piloted himself. Attempting the long cross country trip in dense fog made the Grand National pale into insignificance when after loosing total equilibrium, he suddenly realised he'd been flying upside down for some time.

Thankfully, he righted the machine to land at Plymouth intact. Ironically, a nasty racecourse fall early in 1937 almost achieved what had been averted in the air when Anthony broke his neck and almost certainly that injury contributed to his death while swimming thirteen years on.

That same year Peter Cazalet's riding career ended when a fall at the Military meeting broke an arm so badly he could not resume his former strength.

Davy Jones recovered from leg trouble to continue his winning ways at Gatwick only to go lame again. He was retired to stud at Fairlawne then, when the war broke out, joined the famous Barleythorpe Stud at Oakham in Leicestershire where he saw out his days.

It was not uncommon then for entires to race over fences and only two years after Davy Jones' unlucky departure from the National, the American owned entire Battleship won the 1938 Grand National by a head in a pulsating finish.

As with people from all walks of life, the Second World War changed Anthony Mildmay and Peter Cazalet's well regulated world. They went separate ways to begin with then met up in The Welsh Guards.

There is little doubt when a bazooka shell sliced clean through his tank inches above his head and when a bullet smashed one earphone, Davy Jones' Aintree exploits must have diminished somewhat.

As the war looked ever likely to end during 1944, Cazalet and Mildmay plotted their future which basically centred around Fairlawne with a view to building on their pre-war success. They agreed winning the National came highest on the list.

Armed with a selection of horses for sale from Irish dealer Frank More O'Ferrall, Cazalet bought Watchit and The Frog to start the ball rolling again. Anthony Mildmay whose demob came a few months later chose Newmarket December Sales for his first purchase when securing Fisherman's Yarn from King George.

Mildmay got caught up in the post war euphoria and was prompted to pay far more for his new horse than he normally might have. A large bet on himself first time out covered the outlay.

Determined to improve his riding ability the forerunner of today's mechanical horses was constructed by the Flete Estate carpenter, on which the keen amateur honed his style and strengthened his riding

Lord Mildmay shows Princess Margaret around Buckfastleigh racecourse.

muscles. Those of you unaccustomed to riding horses will be unaware that the sport calls on muscles that you could never have believed existed.

1946/7 saw the friends take giant strides within the steeplechasing game, Cazalet 40 winners, Mildmay 32 from less than a hundred mounts, a record any gentleman rider would find difficult to attain.

That same year saw Anthony's father pass away elevating the popular sportsman to the title of Lord Mildmay. 'Come on M'lord' became the punter's shout as he fought for winners.

The following season Anthony badly injured his neck when falling on hard going at Folkestone. A month later the injury reoccured and forced him to complete the course at Ludlow. after jumping the first, with his neck seized solid.

Despite this inconvenience Lord Mildmay had a real glimmer of hope in the shape of Cromwell, who won three races in a row then elevated himself to a truly potential Grand National type by taking The Manifesto Chase under Cazalet's stable jockey Tony Grantham, the father of today's professional Tom.

Come the Aintree spectacular Cromwell's owner was back on board determined to erase the memory of the Davy Jones debacle. The pair started at 33/1, which in this race is a relatively fancied contender. Kicked at the start and sluggish in the early stages Cromwell proved a very different Aintree partner to the front running, bold jumping Davy Jones.

Passing the grandstands with one circuit and the feared Chair fence behind them, Cromwell had crept up to eleventh place and had warmed to the task. By the 24th fence, the right angled Canal Turn, they had reached the leaders with a full head of steam. Visions of what might happen were at the forefront of the rider's mind yet the seizing up of his neck from the Folkestone fall did not feature among them. Sadly, that is exactly what did happen and from there on in Anthony Mildmay could offer little if any assistance to Cromwell and at that stage of the marathon help from the saddle counts double. The cramp increased to lock the jockeys neck causing him to see nothing but the Aintree turf flying beneath his eyes.

In the event the pair did remarkably well to retain third place behind Sheila's Cottage and Last of The Dandies and must rate equally unlucky as the same connections' Davy Jones twelve years earlier.

Lord Mildmay did manage to win at Aintree when his Irish buy Lecale Prince took the Sefton Chase and in doing so had Dick Francis in his shadow in second place. Once again future racing links were emerging as this was Dick's first venture over the National fences. He became Cazalet's stable jockey and will forever be emblazoned in racegoer's minds as the key player in Her Majesty's racing life. Four hundred plus winners may be a record but that 1956 Grand National will be relived for ever.

Sadly Lecale Prince broke his back when clear of the field in the Topham Trophy.

Cromwell lined up for the National as favourite after his bold showing the year before. Nothing went wrong this time except that he failed to quicken eventually finishing fourth behind the 66/1 shot Russian Hero, who was not surprisingly napped by the racing correspondent of the communist paper the Daily Worker.

The Queen Mother precedes the Queen at Cheltenham racecourse in the Anthony Mildmay era. *(Cheltenham Newspaper Company)*

1949/50 was destined to be the last season Anthony Mildmay rode and was also the time when his infectious enthusiasm for steeplechasing spread to Queen Elizabeth prompting her involvement that has lasted for 45 years.

Although the valiant Cromwell became the victim of another horse on the first circuit in the Grand National, in his final term Anthony Mildmay's riding reached new heights when skillfully outriding both Martin Malony and Arthur Freeman on separate occasions. The former tall, weak amateur had matured into a rider able to hold his own in top professional company.

A unique photo of two doyens of the turf, Mr Jim Joel and The Queen Mother at Sandown in November 1990. Like the Queen Mother he had owned horses for over four decades until his death in 1992. *(Gerry Cranham)*

Lord Mildmay

Lord Mildmay left his mark on racing in no uncertain fashion, modest, happy, quizzically resolute, he was the exemplar of a brave and honourable tradition. There never was a harder rider, a better loser or a more popular winner. Those last two attributes surely have also applied to Queen Elizabeth whose ardent support of the winter game has seen the spark ignited by him fanned into a shining example to all racehorse owners.

Chapter 4

Testing the water: Monaveen does the trick

After the war Peter Cazalet and Lord Mildmay had set out to make Fairlawne into a quality stable and both had the right connections to call upon.

Lord Lewes, who later became The Marquis of Abergavenney and also racing manager to Queen Elizabeth, joined the impressive, expanding list of horse owners, although he was considered an unlucky man in this respect as his horses rarely reached their considerable potential.

King George VI also sent a quirky flat racer to Fairlawne from Captain Cecil Boyd-Rochfort though it was considered prudent to run him in Cazalet's name until such a time that Billposter proved his aptitude for the winter sport.

He had shown his mischievousness on numerous occasions when pulling himself up in the middle of a gallop without warning. This abrupt change of pace usually rid Billposter of his work rider, a game the horse knew he could win every time.

Such a challenge from the King of England made everyone keen to rise to the occasion, especially when his first week under Cazalet's care saw the colt play his hand. He simply refused to move when Jim Fairgrieve mounted, then when the rider gave him a slap to show who was boss, Billposter calmly turned his head and grabbed Jim's boot, they both then understood who held command!

Two strategies altered Billposter's thinking, he underwent complete rebreaking and probably more important, was gelded.

In the trainer's colours the reformed character finished second at Folkestone on his jumping debut, won at Fontwell and four days later again finished second, this time at Cheltenham. A slight tendon strain sealed his fate and Billposter changed hands at Newmarket sales without ever sporting The King's colours from Fairlawne. Although against the Rules of racing for a horse to run in other than the proper owner's name, there are still quite a few horses who run in trainers or their wives names. If you could get evens about them being owned by someone else, there would be no need to attempt to back horses to win races.

Fairlawne, Kent seat of Major Peter Cazalet, Queen Elizabeth's trainer

As so often in this story spanning five decades, families and individuals keep cropping up in different guises and in July of 1948 a young, conscientious amateur, John Oxley joined Fairlawne. He went on to become a successful trainer at Newmarket but as you will read much later on, his son Gerald got the call to wear the blue and buff to some incredible victories.

The next year the French connection produced a batch of horses that were to put Fairlawne on racing's map, including the entire, Manicou, who later not only raced for Queen Elizabeth but then sired three individual winners for her who between them contributed thirty successes.

The date this story of racing longevity and laughter, triumphs and disaster, started was the 22nd July 1949 when Queen Elizabeth and her daughter Princess Elizabeth's chaser Monaveen arrived at Fairlawne.

The gelding had the same sire as Lord Mildmay's National ride Cromwell and another decent inmate, Early Breeze, but he had been purchased primarily on the advice of the stable jockey Tony Grantham.

Tony had come in for a spare ride on the chaser in the 1948 Grand National after a double dose of bad luck for the horse's regular rider, Martin Malony, and then his replacement Vince Mooney, both of whom were injured.

Richard Dunwoody's grandfather, Peter Thrale, trained Monaveen at Epsom and it was not until Tony Grantham got the leg up on him in the Aintree parade ring that he first set eyes on the horse. "The moment we jumped the first fence I knew Monaveen would give me the ride of a lifetime and he did, finishing fifth without touching a twig.

It occurred to me that as the horse had proved himself, he would be ideal to start Queen Elizabeth off in this new sport to her. There is a lot of pressure on someone suggesting a purchase for a Queen but Monaveen had more going for him than most.

By the time we got him his early history had been ironed out. Monaveen had been such a wayward character his Irish owner reputedly straightened out his quirks with a spell pulling a cart in Co. Meath before passing through Goff's sale ring for the princely sum of 90 Gns as a three year old."

By the time he was ready to race for his new owners, Queen Elizabeth had decided to run the chaser in her daughter's livery of scarlet, purple hooped sleeves and a black cap.

Monaveen first appeared at the picturesque Sussex course at Fontwell on October 10th and as Major Cazalet thought the gelding was a little short of peak fitness the decision to hold him up instead of allowing him to bowl along in the lead, made the contest all the more exciting for Princess Elizabeth who witnessed the event. "Even before the race Princess Elizabeth showed a great deal of excitement about the new venture and afterwards she really got caught up in the general euphoria of the occasion. I must say I was a relieved man that nothing silly went wrong," winning jockey Tony Grantham reflected.

Six weeks later a second win, this time at upmarket Sandown Park which features largely in the overall story, Monaveen led from the start and was never once headed.

"The Major told me not to disappoint the horse now that he was fully fit. If it turned out to be half as exhilarating for his owners as it was for me, they will remember the race to this day. He stood off so far in front of the first fence that had anyone measured it, I'm convinced it would have been a record. Often when a horse is as bold as that they struggle to clear the fence yet Monaveen landed just as far the other side. You cannot buy those moments, you have to be lucky enough to have earned the right."

His third victory proved to be most appropriate as the Royal chaser lined up for the inaugural running of The Queen Elizabeth Chase at Hurst Park.

The Queen, as she was at that time, could not be present owing to public duties but Princess Elizabeth, who had flown home from Malta, where her husband Prince Philip was serving in the destroyer H.M.S. Chequers, was a clearly elated spectator. Monaveen's next major target was the 1950 Grand National.

To the delight of the Aintree crowd the King, who had been in poor health, was able to travel to Liverpool with the Queen, the two Princesses and the Duchess of Kent to watch the race from Lord Sefton's box. The Royal party saw Monaveen, a well supported 14/1 chance in the 49 horse field, blaze the trail in flamboyant style before making a comprehensive hash of the fourteenth fence. His rider Tony Grantham, did well to survive it and regain his irons before jumping the next of the thirty obstacles. But the impact took a heavy toll on Monaveen's strength and from there on he was always fighting a losing battle, ultimately finishing fifth of only seven to complete the course. Still it was a fine effort, inspiring the Queen Mother to write to Peter Cazalet, "He must be a great hearted horse".

Sadly, nine months later he would have heavy hearted owners.

Monaveen, Queen Elizabeth's first racehorse, jumping the last to finish 5th in the 1950 Grand National. Tony Grantham on board.

Monaveen who had won four races in the Royal colours before returning to Hurst Park in a bid to win the Queen Elizabeth Chase in successive years was fulfiling his customary front running tactic when he over jumped at the water and shattered a leg so badly that he had to be destroyed immediately.

The bravery that had served Monaveen so well when taking off to jump while his rivals put in another stride, on this occasion proved his demise. Tony Grantham remembered he'd done the same thing at home when schooling. The horse's attribute worked against him.

The Princess was not present on the sad occasion as she was abroad. For the Queen Mother it was a melancholy flight back to Sandringham. Early in her second year of ownership her racing manager Antony Mildmay, had been tragically drowned; now she experienced the sadness of losing a brave horse. For some the sport may have forfeited a little of its appeal. For the Royal patron of Fairlawne it was more than ever a time when Peter Cazalet, a long time friend of the family, and all his staff needed her support.

Her majesty's colours (Blue, buff stripes, blue sleeves, black cap and gold tassel) registered in 1950, were those of her great uncle Lord Strathmore, an outstanding amateur in his time who rode in four successive Grand Nationals between 1847 and 1850.

The first horse to carry Queen Elizabeth's own colours was the French horse Manicou who had been bequeathed, with the rest of his horses, by Anthony Mildmay to Peter Cazalet, was passed on to the Queen Mother.

The first time Queen Elizabeth saw her new acquisition came at Kempton Park where she ran an eye over her recently registered colours only to remark, "The Blue is not quite Royal enough and that is because they have been copied from a set fifty years old in which the blue has faded. In time I intend to have a new set and this time the blue will be truly blue."

Queen Elizabeth had shown stamina to match her bold chaser's, having been still dancing at 3 a.m. after a State banquet for Queen Juliana and Prince Bernhard of the Netherlands at Buckingham Palace. She was fifty years of age then and having done so many times since, again led the Conga at a house party at 3.30 a.m. the morning of the Hennessey Gold Cup only four years ago. Queen Elizabeth simply radiates life and the fact that she has remained involved in steeplechasing for 45 years has provided the best possible encouragement to others.

Injuries sustained by Tony Grantham at Hurst Park kept him out of action for two months. There was, as ever, a thoughtful message for him from the owner when that fine rider Bryan Marshall took over on Manicou in mid December at Sandown, where the young horse was so impressive in the Ewell Handicap Chase that it was decided to have a crack at Kempton's prestigious King George VI Chase. The only five year old in the high class, seven horse line up which included two subsequent Gold Cup winners, Manicou and Marshall scored a famous victory. The Boxing Day crowd loved it.

"I'll be back in time to win the Gold Cup on him," insisted Tony Grantham. He was too. But by then (25 April 1951) the Royal chaser had completely lost his form - he finished last of six and never did recover his old form. In fact it proved to be a further 34 years before Queen Elizabeth won another chase of similar standing when Special Cargo snatched the 1984 Whitbread Gold Cup with the very last possible stride.

Bryan Marshall wins the King George VI Chase on the entire Manicou for the Queen Mother in 1950, only a year after owning her first racehorse. Dick Francis is second on Silver Fame.

After a series of set backs the Queen Mother had Manicou home at Sandringham for a long break. However, when returned into training unsoundness recurred repeatedly and, three years on from his glory day, it had to be accepted that Manicou's racing life was ended. Happily, as an 'entire', he still had a future and since the Queen Mother rarely sells a horse who has been in her service, preferring to find a suitable home or care for him herself, Manicou was placed as a stallion with Mr Charles Godden in Sussex.

For Tony Grantham who had the honour of starting Queen Elizabeth off on the winning trail, the sacking of Bryan Marshall by Dorothy Paget meant a change in the pecking order as Peter Cazalet started to put Marshall up on what would have been previously Tony's rides.

Although he continued to ride the horses at exercise and still part-nered some Cazalet trained horses on the course, it was a case of the crumbs not the main meal.

Accumulated injuries forced Tony Grantham out of the game in 1958. He eventually retired to Ireland where with Sally his wife, they have a few young horses about the place, train several point to pointers and also keep their ties with England by having a couple in training with Jim Old and Robert Alner.

The pace of life on their stud in Co. Clare not far from Shannon Airport suits the now seventy year old Grantham whose memory of those first five Royal winners is razor sharp. His professional jockey son Tom, today provides the link with the life that Tony Grantham would not swap for the sole winning ticket in Saturday's lottery.

The gap in Queen Elizabeth's winners from Manicou in 1950 to M'As-Tu-Vu three years later is explained by her horses recovering from lameness, a period of mourning for King George VI and adjustment after the coronation of her daughter as Sovereign.

Dick Francis had then been lured to the stable by the impressive rate of increased quality and quantity winners under the Cazalet banner. He shared M'As-Tu-Vu's six successes with Arthur Freeman but it was the trainer's own point to pointer Willie Hayes that gave him his biggest thrill at that time.

Head Lad Jim Fairgreave had been warned the owner would be there incognito, a cloth cap replacing the usual Bowler. "I'm not coming near you," he told Jim, "You saddle up and I'll back him for you."

The whole episode was so out of character yet the plot gave all concerned a great deal of satisfaction. Cazalet was landed gentry and fastidious regarding the right thing to do in any circumstances yet the thought of landing a small betting coup at a Point to Point really sent a surge of blood through his veins, and that is one of the reasons that the turf attracts its followers.

Queen Elizabeth felt at ease at Fairlawne. She had been a regular visitor there as a teenage girl when close friends with Peter Cazalet's sister Thelma Cazalet-Keer. Her name in the visitors book bears testimony to the frequency of her jaunts eighty years ago. Thelma Cazalet-Keer served as under minister in the Churchill Administration during the war.

Queen Elizabeth wrote of those happy carefree days to Peter Cazalet's son Edward after his aunt's death.

He also well remembers Queen Elizabeth's visits starting up again when becoming a patron of the stable in 1949. "She so loves genuine characters and the stories they can tell and then became equally interested in the horses that seem to draw these people to them. My father had a very good sense of humour which he shared with Queen Elizabeth. They had lots of in jokes. She liked to play croquet here, walk around the grounds and gardens and loved to go around all the horses in the stables or watch them cantering.

Every December my step mother invited a large amount of people to stay when Queen Elizabeth came down for Lingfield races. Albert Roux cooked for us on this weekend for nine consecutive years. Zara planned the guest list to ensure three days of entertainment and invariably asked a celebrity or two from the world of showbusiness. People like Noel Coward or Chan Canasta made an ideal mix with the few racing buffs invited. Even when blowing or sleeting the weather could not stop Queen Elizabeth watching the horses work. Her head would be facing the gallops, enjoying every minute of it. Noel Coward on the other hand failed to find the same enthusiasm."

Edward's step mother Zara Cazalet adds, "Queen Elizabeth has a naturally high body temperature which is why she always wears open necked coats and dresses whatever the weather even now in her 95th year.

She called Peter 'The Fuhrer' because he bossed her around in the same way he ran the stables. Peter was the most wonderful man and wonderful character but absolutely rigid although I never saw any hardness in him. I always say so few people have been married to the only person they've really loved. That was my luck in life, lucky is an understatement."

Edward Cazalet takes up the story, "Come what may father made sure that we had a mass of runners at Lingfield. The place was prone to flooding though and one year I distinctly remember him phoning Peter Beckwith Smith with raised voice when we had Queen Elizabeth staying and intending to race a double handful, 'We simply have to race Peter, it doesn't matter if we have to swim the horses we're racing!!!' He insisted on making this weekend fun for Queen Elizabeth with a concert pianist or film show after the racing.

My father knew how much his Royal patron loved racecourse action and on reflection there is no doubt the horses ran more often than they should have done. I spent several seasons riding out for Ryan Price and could see he laid a horse out for specific race in the year whereas ours ran every two weeks providing they were sound. We invariably had a flow of winners up to Christmas each year, then having given their all, we had disappointments at the Cheltenham Festival. He had the horses fit to race in September each season so that they were in peak condition when Queen Elizabeth came down from her annual holiday in Scotland. I think there was a fair amount of adjustment to fit her timetable which was the only concession my father made.

He and Anthony Mildmay were determined to put National Hunt on the map as it had always been the poor relation to the flat. To some extent they succeeded and by encouraging Queen Elizabeth to come into the sport, they made a lot of people write and talk about the game. It was a tremendous step forward.

Father always said you need someone to share the fun, have some laughs and mull over the disappointments. When Antony Mildmay died he was berefit and then his growing racing involvement with Queen Elizabeth played some compensatory part.

At one stage she had a string of 25 horses at Fairlawne and it amazed me how much she knew about not only her own, but also the others.

She has an eye for it, and can tell at a glance if one is well or below par. What is more she even likes to feel their legs for signs of trouble, doing so in the fashion of a horsemaster. She has the way of touching horses that only truly knowledgeable people have.

I realised there are a limited number of horses owners who genuinely get a kick when their horse is in with a chance two fences from home. Queen Elizabeth does, and to my mind that sorts out those who really love racing from those who have horses just for social reasons."

Edward Cazalet is himself an accomplished rider with 70 point to point winner and 25 on the racecourse. None were gained in the Royal colours, although he did get one shot at achieving every jump jockeys ambition when as a last minute replacement at Hurst Park for Double Star's regular rider who had been injured.

The haste of the changed circumstances left the amateur jockey unaware of the horse's habit of totally ignoring one fence in every race, Edward did well to retain the partnership and only just gave best to the aptly named Certain Justice.

He could have pursued his race riding interests while working as a lawyer but listened to his father who reasoned people would not take him seriously if he were seen riding at Sandown Park mid week. It could and would destroy a practice.

On his father's death it was Edward's decision to continue his legal path and end the training era that had been his father's life. Fairlawne's racing history belonged to the father not the son.

For the past 22 years Mr Justice Cazalet, High Court Judge, has got his weekly adrenaline flush as master of the Mid Surrey Farmers' Drag Hunt.

He reasons it is a very sedentary life being in the law, total sedentary as a judge, sitting there for five and a half hours every day without being able to move your arms about. "I need to do something mad on a Saturday and I can assure you we jump some pretty sizable obstacles."

Fairlawne became the home of Prince Khalid Abdullah whose racing interests have been totally geared to the flat with remarkable success. His studs and trainers operate elsewhere with the sounds of hooves in

The Queen Mother, then Queen Elizabeth, watching the racing at close quarters in the centre of Prestbury Park in 1953. The first picture Royal racing photographer, Bernard Parkin took of the Queen Mother. *(Bernard Parkin)*

the historic home stables a rarity. The house has been renovated internally to Royal standards without changing the outward appearance although some of the more mature parkland trees have fallen foul to the storms. It remains shrouded in racing history though, and will be remembered for the active part it played in this story.

However, I have leaped too far too fast because Devon Loch and others are about to fire the owner's interest at Fairlawne in the mid 1950's.

Chapter 5

Devon Loch: A bitter pill

New horse owners to the jumping game often have to wait years for success while others find a big winner straight away. Queen Elizabeth had enjoyed a good start with Monaveen and Manicou then the Irish bred Devon Loch looked as if he would pluck the choicest race for her, only to witness an incredible happening snatch Grand National victory from her grasp.

The chaser had given head lad Jim Fairgrieve a few grey hairs within two days of joining the stable when the buckle of the lunge rein broke, freeing the new inmate who promptly disappeared through the park, jumped a set of rails and came to a halt in a neighbour's field. Usually horses that manage to stay uninjured after such a freedom flight turn out to be utterly useless, the good ones seem to get hurt. Devon Loch proved the exception to that rule.

Bryan Marshall held court at the time he started winning as Dick Francis opted to ride the stables better fancied Lochroe and Arthur Freeman took the second choice, At Bay.

Peter Cazalet's orders to Marshall were to look after himself and make sure he got the horse around the course in one piece. Should he be able to finish third, everyone would be pleased, indicating that was the best they could hope for. In the event Lochroe never fired at all, At Bay hit the deck and Devon Loch responded to a typical Marshall ride when nursed until the last fence had been negotiated only to produce a surprising burst of speed to thrill both The Queen and her mother who were in attendance.

As with ninety percent of jump jockeys Bryan Marshall had few front teeth of his own due to the inevitable and frequent falls. Conscious of his facial situation, Bryan chose to wear his false teeth whenever Queen Elizabeth attended the races. Aware of the dangers of riding with dentures in place he sought the assistance of Devon Loch's lad John Hole to wrap them in his handkerchief as they left the parade ring and return them to the jockey the moment Marshall pulled up after the finishing post.

"I know what you're up to," the Queen Mother tells Bryan Marshall, who tried to hide his actions when putting in his false teeth. (l to r; The Queen, Lord Abergavenny, The Queen Mother, Bryan Marshall, Peter Cazalet and Bill Braddon)

Queen Elizabeth became aware of this ploy and always ready to join in with the fun, caught him on the hop at Hurst Park. She saw him slide his hand over his mouth transferring the teeth from cupped hand to mouth and said with a laugh, "I know exactly what you have in your hand!" and as everyone around was in on the act, they all burst into spontaneous laughter.

Marshall partnered Devon Loch to one further win at Sandown Park the next month. He had reported then that the horse had twice given him an unusual 'feel', he faltered for a few strides, got a second wind and set sail for home. Although unable to decipher what those signs indicated, it may hold the key to his sudden malfunction in the National.

Marshall deferred to the stable jockey Dick Francis for the 1955/56 season and in all Dick enjoyed four victories on Devon Loch and finished second on him in the King George VI Chase but it is the National that makes his story so different from the other Royal horses.

To this day Devon Loch's rider Dick Francis is adamant the gelding reacted so dramatically to the wave of sound from the tens of thousands of spectators that he recoiled and sprawled to the ground with only fifty yards to cover of the four and a half mile race.

Others close to the horse are of different opinions but no one will ever know for certain what caused such a travesty of justice. To have survived those 30 tricky fences, avoided falling and lose rivals and to be actually pulling clear of the closest pursuer with only 50 yards to run, would be enough to win any other Grand National since its inception.

Peter Cazalet's son Edward, who was riding at a point to point that day, received a garbled message that his father had won the National for The Queen Mother. Having seen the race numerous times since on film he is convinced the rider may not be the best person to evaluate the cause and is himself of the opinion Devon Loch saw the water jump and tried to jump it from instinct. I heartily concur with that theory, although it is of little matter now why or how the result of the 1956 Grand National changed, suffice to know it did. E.S.B. won the race under Dave Dick for Worcester trainer Fred Rimell and owner Mrs Leonard Carver.

Head lad Jim Fairgrieve stayed in London the night before the National unable to sleep, he knew Devon Loch could win alright but had an inexplicable, unnerving feeling within himself. This premonition persisted all throughout the train journey to Aintree. By the time Devon Loch had pulled 10 lengths clear and only had 50 routine yards to gallop the uneasy feeling had evaporated.

Jim was off the stands and running to greet his charge when the roars turned to moans and the awful truth hit home.

In Lord Sefton's private viewing box a section of the Royal party were still openly cheering as others started to react to what was happening. Of the front row guests, Princess Margaret, The Queen (four years into her reign, displayed open mouthed emotion that the passing years have happily failed to quell), Zara and Peter Cazalet plus The Queen Mother were jubilant while in their midst the Princess Royal was first to spot the terrible outcome erupting.

The manner in which The Queen Mother both consoled the distraught Dick Francis and also presented the trophy to the winners with grace and charm, speaks volumes for her strength of character, breeding and upbringing.

While Peter Cazalet left the Royal party to discuss matters with Dick Francis, Lord Abergavenny who had succeeded Lord Mildmay as The Queen Mother's racing manager, asked Fairgrieve to accompany The Queen Mother and Princess Margaret to the stables where Devon Loch looked totally recovered. His owner only had thoughts for the horse, her own emotions saved for more private moments. "I'll have an ache in my heart for ever," she later wrote to Peter Cazalet.

His wife Zara remembers walking out with Peter Beckwith-Smith who remarked, "You would not have known anything had happened, your husband's self control and that of all the Royals was an example to everyone". They went back to stay with Bunny and Gina Phillips who reported in the privacy of the house they were all very, very low.

The next day Peter Cazalet met Jim Fairgrieve in the Fairlawne office after the morning church service to do the list of who rode what the next day. He looked at his number one man, gave him a quizzical smile and said "We must try again Jim".

The National Press demanded post race pictures to which Peter Cazalet agreed would at least show the public the horse was alive and well. One hard nosed newshound then learned a lesson he'll still remember having asked if the trainer could make Devon Loch do the splits for his photographer exactly as he had done two days before at Aintree!

Queen Elizabeth sent her distraught trainer a cigarette box "as a memento of that terrible and yet glorious day last Saturday. Glorious because of Devon Loch's magnificent performance and terrible

Devon Loch collapses with only 50 yards to the finish. Dave Dick on E.S.B. passes to win the 1956 Grand National, while a disconsolate Dick Francis cannot believe what has happened. *(Sunday Express)*

because of that unprecedented disaster when victory seemed so sure. We must now pray that such a gallant horse will go on to another great race, perhaps next year. I am sure that you know how deeply I feel for you and I can understand a little of the anguish you must have felt at such a cruel blow. I send my heartfelt sympathy to you and all at Fairlawne. We will not be done in by this, and will just keep trying."

Zara Cazalet affirms the owner and trainer never once showed their private grief in public, although it was then and is still now brought up spasmodically. She also recounts how the innocence of youth is such a leveler. "I was pregnant with my third Cazalet child in 1956, the baby who actually died. When we got back home, Victor who was then four and Anthony, two, had been told of the terrible happening. They set about making and then racing over a range of fences around the day nursery saying 'I'm Devon Loch and I'm winning, I'm winning'. Peter and I just exchanged wry smiles and agreed we'd never be allowed to forget it.

You must remember he had seen Davy Jones run out at the last fence with the National at his mercy and Cromwell placed with his rider Anthony Mildmay unable to help the horse over the last mile having been paralysed with neck cramp. Those incidents he put behind him but he never did get over Devon Loch's downfall."

Dick Francis partnered eleven winners for The Queen Mother, five of them on Devon Loch but it is the events of the 1956 Grand National that have immortalised him in racegoer's memories. Who knows, those awful happenings may also be responsible for his worldwide acclaim as a racing fiction writer. Dick wrote his autobiography titled The Sport of Queens a year later and since Dead Cert his first fiction in 1962 has never missed topping the charts with a novel each year.

Often in life, chance meetings generate hitherto unconsidered avenues and one such good turn pushed Dick to swap the whip for a pen. Literary agent John Johnson had taken his elderly mother to tea with Dick's mother barely two months after the National and while there he remarked on a framed photograph of Devon Loch jumping the last Aintree fence unaware of the connection. He followed up that lead prompting Dick to decline the offer of a ghost writer and buckle down to the task himself while on a boat on the Norfolk Broads.

Although continuing to race ride for the first six months of the

1956/57 season, Dick retired in February 1957 following a nasty fall at Newbury. Lord Abergavenny encouraged him to surprise people with the news which they did by engineering the announcement on BBC's Sportsview program. It had the desired effect with an immediate approach of three job offers. The two within racing as a judge and race commentator did not sit easily on Dick's shoulders whereas writing for The Sunday Express and finishing his autobiography proved surprisingly cosy. In retrospect commentating would never have worked for Dick who for such a brilliant writer is a surprisingly moderate public speaker.

It has been suggested he's better known for not winning the National but had he done so for The Queen Mother, his name would have been written in stone.

The Queen Mother is pleased to welcome Devon Loch when he finishes second in the 1956 King George VI Chase, "Winning is a bonus".

All kinds of people were affected by the result of the 1956 Grand National including Colonel Stephen Hill-Dillon who had bought Devon Loch as a two year old off the flat. Recognising potential as a jumper he castrated his 550 Gns purchase and gave him that all important ingredient, time.

He ran from Hill-Dillon's yard for the first time as a five year old, winning at Naas on his next outing. This win promoted Devon Loch as appetising to English buyers of which Peter Cazalet was first to put his hand in his pocket to produce the necessary to make him the property of Queen Elizabeth. Convinced he was selling a chaser of the highest quality, Hill-Dillon managed to include a contingency which would bring him a further £1000 should Devon Loch win The Cheltenham Gold Cup and double that amount if victorious in the Grand National.

Imagine the heady mixture of pride and the thought of his £2000 contingency as Stephen Hill-Dillon witnessed his former horse striding away with the worlds greatest steeplechase only for both emotion and hard cash to disintegrate with the winning post in sight?

The chaser came back the next season to win over hurdles and continued to show the National had no lasting effects by winning another two chases. Dick had been hurt at Newbury letting Arthur Freeman in for the ride on Devon Loch in what turned out to be his last race at Sandown in the Mildmay Memorial Chase where he broke down. Freeman reported the horse had faltered half way up the run in to the extent he almost went down. This could have been due to him breaking down at that point or perhaps it was the same reason he sprawled at Aintree?

Whatever, the horse never ran again and proved superb when given to Sir Noel Murless as a hack to use on Newmarket Heath. He returned to Sandringham to see his days out.

Devon Loch, the first Royal product of the Irish era, prompted a plan where well bred, properly conformed yearlings were inexpensively purchased by Stephen Hill-Dillon, scrutinised and selected by Peter Cazalet and Captain Charles Moore and shipped to Sandringham as two year olds. In all, eleven youngsters were produced along this chain with Gay Record the best of the bunch by a mile.

The idea was sound enough and did give Queen Elizabeth a great deal of pleasure as she monitored their progress from two to four years at the Royal Stud then while being educated by Eldred Wilson before joining Peter Cazalet.

There is no doubt that the chain was made up of very knowledgeable people who had the use of the best of everything needed to bring out their potential. As this failed to happen the buck must rest with the buyer, the other links having proved themselves with countless horses from other sources.

Hill-Dillon had bought numerous successful youngsters for himself and had a proven track record when supplying Lord Bicester with his good chasers plus earning his spurs with Cazalet by recommending Cromwell to him. In the case of the eleven yearlings he must have been trying too hard in view of their Royal destination.

Eldred Wilson became an important part of the Queen Mother's racing team from 1952 when asked to take and break the youngsters. Now 89 years old his memory is enviably sharp. "While talking to King George and the Queen at the 1949 Sandringham Flower Show I suggested they might care to take a break from the annual cricket match by coming to the farm I leased from them to see the show horses and thoroughbreds I kept about the place. It went on from there really."

Eldred's grandfather was already farming Harpley Dams when King George V bought Sandringham from the 3rd Earl of Leicester's Holkham Estate in 1912 and it is only this year that Eldred has moved to a newly built bungalow at nearby Flitcham. Even though this era has ended and there are no longer any horses kept at Harpley Dams, at The Queen's request the two mile long turf gallop that runs the length of the farm has been retained for their own use when hacking about the estate.

He is in every sense an amazing man having started riding in races aged 21 and rode in his last point to point at the age of 70!!

During those years Eldred Wilson partnered all of ninety winners, his horsemanship serving to keep him in one piece in a game that usually bends and breaks participants on a regular basis. He had some falls including in The Foxhunters' Chase at Aintree over the big fences. He lessened the odds against injury by studying Judo and regularly diving over tennis nets to perfect his fall and roll technique. In 49 years of raceriding the galloping Major never broke a bone, perhaps modern day jockeys might be better employed diving over tennis nets instead of trying to hit aces!

Ironically, each of Major Wilson's three best chasers were offered to Peter Cazalet in turn for The Queen Mother but they were all discarded by the trainer. Essandam won 21 chases while River Buoy took 30 first prizes. Horses under his care went through the same learning curve which took in ridden show classes at the Norfolk horse shows and hunting with the West Norfolk Hunt but it was his common sense methods of breaking in youngsters that sticks in the mind most of all.

"You have to realise how much of a shock to young horses it must be when having looked at humans at eye level all their life, they then feel and see riders upon their backs. To get them used to this drastic change of command I'd tie straw filled sacks to a rope suspended from a large beam above the stable. As they moved about their box the sacks would constantly brush across their back and soon it became accepted not alien.

That same suspended rope later played a vital part in my own survival and hastened the process of getting the youngster to yield to the rider's commands. No matter how much preparatory work, most unbroken horses violently object to a rider's presence on their back and staying put becomes a battle of wits. By lowering myself from the rope into the saddle I could increase or lighten the pressure and if one did turn itself inside out, I could pull myself up out of harms way while keeping at least one leg on his back. The bad horses tired of trying to get rid of me long before I did.

My father and grandfather had used the same trick for decades and first introduced me to it aged twelve. They said there were two unbroken ponies in one stable and I was not to come out until I'd managed to stay on both. I lost count of the number of times I swung across the stable on the rope before the ponies succumbed but they did."

Eldred thought the Sandringham horses were rather overfed and under exercised in those days so he chanced his arm when The Rip and Mel joined him, opting to treat his Royal guests the same as his own, reasoning "Steeplechasing is a winter game when they'll work through the worst weather every year, so why not get them hardened to the elements? I winter them out in the fresh air providing shelter and the best of food and a certain amount of minerals. Horses last longer if they are not treated like greenhouse plants.

Right from the first horses I had for Queen Elizabeth it became obvious she was a horsewoman. She noticed and remarked on the fact that The Rip sought out natural herbs in the pasture. He used to forage intently until finding what he was seeking, stay at the same patch until he'd cleared it all up then almost like a bloodhound, would move on to nose out similar growth.

The Queen Mother is also far from a fair weather owner. Numerous Christmas visits were in the snow bordering on blizzard conditions when we were schooling the point to pointers. I'd take shelter behind a straw stack but Her Majesty braved it out always with her head held high not wanting to miss a thing."

Chapter 6

Jack of all Trades and Master of them

A typical example of the Queen Mother's 'hands on' approach to her horseracing came in 1960 when the Royal trainer Peter Cazalet decided he'd exhausted the diverse methods of calming down the wayward Gay Record. Irishman Jack O'Donoghue took on the unenviable task and recalls.

"Major Cazalet suggested the horse be sold and had found a suitable home with a local farmer for the nominal sum of £25. Many of Queen Elizabeth's horses had gone the same route previously when their racing careers waned or they proved too slow for the job they had been bred or purchased for but the owner would not agree with this one as she thought there was a specific reason for his disappointing attitude.

She felt the old fashioned indoor stables that housed the Fairlawne horses made Gay Record feel claustrophobic. Basically, the horse was not happy.

The renowned worrier went back to Sandringham for the summer while the Queen Mother pondered over his future and decided he would benefit from a smaller establishment where there were traditional stables in a square yard enabling the inmates to see what was going on throughout the day.

Major Wilson was asked to present a list from which Queen Elizabeth chooses me and after the initial shock, at first I thought it was a practical joke, I realized I could only do my best. I must say the Queen Mother really became involved with our little stable and often popped down to mix and mingle with the diverse goings on here. I found her and the Queen terribly sensible," Jack observed.

The choice could not have been better as the homely yard housed a multitude of animals to distract the enigmatic Gay Record from thinking about himself. Jack is one of those rare people who understand and love all of God's creatures. Even now with the town of Reigate ever spreading up the hill to the M25, Jack's cottage and stables provide a thriving island of all that is good in life. Although just 100 yards from the humming High Street, you would never know what historic deeds had and are still being hatched within the heart of this London commuter belt town.

Quietly spoken O'Donoghue understands animals of all types. He is famed for his donkeys which have been mopping up the top prizes for showing, driving, racing and jumping them. Yes! Jumping. Many of his home breds have cleared four feet and when you consider how stubborn they are at Fetes and Donkey Derbies, it puts his expertise into prospective. Even now aged 87 Jack's current donkey, Little Record, has amassed an unbelievable total of 170 prizes, earning him a Gold Medal for outstanding success.

"They're great to have around, racehorses are calmed down by them because they have the ability to ignore, even the nastiest tempered horse cannot upset them. When I turn horses out to grass with a donkey they soon stop charging about to pal up with the donkey. It's like human nature really, if you cannot rile a workmate you soon leave him alone and often see the huge benefit of staying calm. My horses spend most of their stabled hours with their heads over the half doors watching the antics of the donkeys, bullocks, pigs and ornamental pheasants I breed. They are entertained all day during the daylight hours and then are pleased to rest at night. If you can get a worrier to forget his work, you'll get the best out of him. Eating and sleeping are just as important as excercise in any walk of life."

Another hobby Jack has been successful at is training bullocks to pull carts, finding the dairy breed of Fresians to be best suited to the shafts. They and the donkeys have long pulled the 'muck barrow' around the yard during daily morning and evening stable cleaning times.

There is such an air of safety within the walled yard that even out-siders such as squirrels sit quite happily on pigs' backs, while horses recuperating after injury mix contentedly with their time honoured pink, grunting enemies.

It was to this environment that the neurotic Gay Record went for therapy and as racing history relates, he loved every minute of it. It could not have been any further removed from the palatial sur-roundings at Fairlawne and its regimented regime.

Training horses is mostly common sense. Finding the right horse and owners to support them are the two most important ingredients to being a successful stable but when it comes down to enticing the problem horse to give it's best, that is when the real horseman's ability comes into play.

As much as Queen Elizabeth loved the weekend visits and the privacy the Fairlawne Estate provided, she also thrived on the involvement O'Donoghue's patch purveyed.

Gay Record had been troublesome from a young age, one of a regular stream of horses bought as yearlings in Ireland. He'd come off worst in a gang fallout at grass, injuring a shin and probably exagger-ating his mental attitude to others.

When joining Major Wilson to grow on and start his education, Gay Record worried even during his spells out hunting in Norfolk, a dis-traction most young horses relish. He was highly strung and remained so, worrying the condition off his frame.

Although given plenty of time to mature before asked to repay some of his owners patience, by the age of six when he went into training with Cazalet, the gelding had not improved his mental state. Travelling prompted sweating to such a degree that he had run two races before ever getting to the start and on one occasion so much steam billowed from the horsebox taking him to the sports that a following motorist flagged it down fearing the motor transporter was on fire.

Three races under Cazalet's care yielded a second at the now defunct Kentish course at Wye. The leaky nervous wreck had ability if the holes in his make up could be plugged.

Jack took his time to evaluate and understand his new challenge with regular playing sessions in the paddock between wayward horse and docile donkey. Determined not to leave any stone unturned, Jack enlisted the help of fellow Cork born Collis Montgomery, a veteran of 120 point to point wins and a legendary horseman.

Collis Montgomery hunting Gay Record with the Surrey Union Hunt to take the horse's mind off racing. *(Ruck Press)*

"I sent for him and he came at once, as delighted with the thought of the challenge as I was", Jack mistily remembers, "Monty had a way with horses, he used to go off hacking all over the place on his own talking to Gay Record for hours on end about everything and anything. The locals in the town thought he had gone mad telling the horse the sort of things you would say to a friend over a pint.

The opposite is true though, the more natural the chat the quicker the horse relates to the tone and there is no doubt they do listen, admittedly more to the tone than the words. When we'd got his confidence, I dispatched Monty and Gay Record off hunting with The Old Surrey & Burstow Hunt. No matter what the weather, they enjoyed a day out together as by then the bond had been cemented.

At Queen Elizabeth's suggestion we sent the horse to local race-courses to school him over fences, with Hurst Park and Kempton favoured as they were only half an hour's journey in the horsesbox. Collis schooled him only a year short of pension age, there's many a man less than half that age would not have done that in cold blood, not even for the Queen.

Two things of importance came out of these away days. Firstly the horse began to think of box journeys as part of life generally and also, arriving at the course held no terrors for him as it had been playtime not work.

When Gay Record got to the course at Fontwell for his first race from our stable he finished second, ironically to a former stablemate, Cazalet's Cupid's Charge. He showed us he'd grown into a man, Collis's job had been done and he decided to move on. Collis was known worldwide having travelled horses for Pedens for years and it was perhaps fitting that when his life was prematurely snuffed out in an air crash at Heathrow, he went out with a bunch of horses. He lived and died among and for them."

Gay Record went to Kempton Park for his follow up run only to end up on the deck when looking as if he'd got them all beat. Disappointing, yes, but the Royal plan was working, the horse could do the job he was bred and purchased for.

Under 'Tumper' Lehane the gelding lost his maiden tag first time out the next season back at Fontwell and although he failed to add to that tally the same term, he was placed often, displaying a stronger consti-tution.

The chaser went from strength to strength, eventually winning nine races and being placed second more than twenty times. O'Donoghue had proved more than up to the Royal calling.

Gene Kelly followed Tumper into Gay Record's saddle and the new pairing gelled well. It has meant a great deal to him with the original set of Blue and Buff royal silks hanging proudly at his home near Broadway. "We used to share them with Major Cazalet then a new set arrived and somehow I ended up with the old ones." Kelly smiles, "Do you know, The Queen Mother remembers names and faces even after years. I was showing sheep at a recent Smithfield Show where Her Majesty wins prizes for both cattle and sheep and as she passed along the exhibitors she spotted me and stopped to say Hello, calling me by

Jack O'Donoghue has an affinity with all animals. Gay Record mixes quite happily.

name and that after all these years." (Perhaps she was getting around to asking for her colours back Gene).

"At Windsor after Gay Record had smashed the course record with one racing plate sticking out several inches from his hoof having trodden on it with his other foot, we were waiting at the exit gate to take our leave when The Queen Mother put her hand out to shake Jack's. He'd been holding the twisted metal shoe inside his pocket and when he withdrew it to acknowledge the offered hand, the metal shoe came with it and there it was pressed firmly between their hands prompting genuine laughter from Queen Elizabeth."

Among those victories a milestone was passed that now seems small in comparison with the happenings since. The aptly named Gay Record notched up the one hundred mark, yet as Peter Cazalet had 15 of the Queen Mother's jumpers under his care to Jack O'Donoghue's 4, the odds were stacked against the homely Reigate stable producing the one that mattered.

Of the four, three were either sick, lame or slow, with only Gay Record able to fly the O'Donoghue flag.

It had been fifteen years since Queen Elizabeth started out with a shared racehorse. Many time we read in the racing Press that an owner has just witnessed his or her first winner after twenty years of trying.

We are quite used to mild, dry autumn's these days, but in 1964 the dry, hard ground extended long after the change of daylight hours and the fields were sadly depleted. The O'Donoghue stable had the cough to thwart its mission too and even by the 20th of October Gay Record had not stretched his legs in public.

"The old horse could not shake off the cough whatever we gave him until it got to the stage of spasmodic rasps rather than persistent barks. I'd entered him for a moderate race at Folkestone in case he shook it off and even though it remained with him on the morning of the race we decided to let him take his chance. It's not unlike a car that is stuttering along, give it a burn up and it clears the passages. The horse had no temperature so I knew he was not ill.

Only three horses lined up with our fellow starting odds on to win. Gene Kelly was off injured so I engaged Bobby Beasley to ride; he's one of the most stylish riders I've seen.

Disproving the theory, that donkey's do not jump!

Little Record had to earn his corn too, pulling the muck barrow!

When the result matters as much as this one did and taking into consideration the fact that I had taken a chance by running him at all, the nerves were stretched to breaking point. T'is a terrible thing to have to watch horses race from the stands when you have witnessed so many happenings from the saddle. T'is agony not to have any charge over proceedings once the tapes fly up and they are running. I couldn't watch, instead I sloped off behind the stands and listened to the commentary. T'is an awful lonely place and the changes that go on in the mind and body during that seven minute race would not be experienced by laymen in a year.

Bobby told me afterwards the old horse jumped brilliantly, made the running except for half a mile and took the owner to the century of winners decisively. I was a mightily relieved man and felt drained as if I'd run the marathon."

The Queen Mother had not come back from her annual Balmoral holiday in Scotland but the phone lines between owner and trainer were long engaged and before Jack had got back to settle his horse in with a hot linseed mash for the night, a congratulatory telegram from Queen Elizabeth sat waiting in Priory Cottage.

Everyone who has had the privilege of working for The Queen Mother has remarked that she invariably is more pleased for them than for herself. A silver ashtray engraved and signed by the owner serve to remind the 87 year old O'Donoghue of his place in this Royal record. His eyes mist over then as his incredibly sharp mind recalls every detail including the celebratory at The Savoy. "Besides congratulating me on the win, Queen Elizabeth danced with me and every one else there too. She stayed the trip alright, the party went on to 4 a.m. and she was going as strongly then as anyone."

The family turned out in force as they still do for these informal dinners with the horse world.

When Gay Record reached the century he was the Queen Mother's first winner since Makaldar had done likewise at Haydock Park in Lancashire eight months earlier, but having brought the drought to an end he then featured in another day to remember when the middle leg of a Folkstone treble two weeks later.

It has long been one of steeplechasing's most endearing charms that the smallest team can topple the mightiest battalions.

Big is not best although we do become brainwashed into believing the stables that produce the most winners are the best.

Fine recent examples of this are the victories of dairy farmer Syrill Griffiths lifting The Tote Gold Cup with his 100/1 outsider Norton's Coin, permit holder Henry Cole's succession of major chases victories with his home bred mare Dubacilla and her brother Just So who finished second in the 1994 Martell Grand National. That same race witnessed fifty-one year old housewife Rosemary Henderson train and ride her ex-cripple, Fiddlers Pike into fifth place. Like O'Donoghue these trainers have shown they can extricate the very best from the material at their disposal. Most choose not to enlarge their string as that in itself destroys the very thing they are in the sport for, fun!

Conversely, many of record breaker Martin Pipe's cleverest successes have been gained in small races with horses of extremely limited ability and numerous physical problems.

Jack had sprung to racing prominence in 1951 when producing the former cripple Nickel Coin to win the Grand National, the last mare to have triumphed in this greatest of all steeplchasing tests. As a foal the tiny filly could not get to her feet and despite being bottle fed was still unable to rise after ten days, prompting her breeder Mr R. Corbet to instruct his vet to humanely destroy the weakling.

On overhearing this, the housekeeper threatened him with her resignation should the instruction go ahead and not being disposed to loosing a good housekeeper, the foal was saved. She was reared on a mattress in front of the staff kitchen Aga. Splints were fitted to her frail legs and with the help of the estate's grooms, the little foal was helped to its feet daily and, happily, it responded to the tender loving care.

As a yearling the filly went through the sale ring at Newmarket and was knocked down to Jack's patron Jeffrey Royle for the princely sum of 50 Gns. Who could have foreseen that he would be handling the real Royal horses a decade later?

Mr Royle, who divided his time between Shropshire and Surrey took a 300 Gns profit on the filly two years later then bought her back again at the age of five, only to take a second profit almost straight away.

Nickel Coin went to work then winning five open show jumping championships before the intrepid dealer Mr Royle once more became

A line of promising Royal chasers at Jack O'Donoghue's yard in 1964.
(l to r; Carragheen, National Emblem, Sunbridge, Manicola, Augustine and Gay
Record)

Paddy O'Brien, J. O'Donoghue up, winning the Heavyweight race from Antrim II,
at a point to point at Gatwick in 1948. (This was the last ever race meeting held
at Gatwick)

her owner when she was seven.

The state of play was much the same as it had been six years previously except that Jeffrey Royle had made £500 on his exchanges and still owned the mare.

Jack had long been a believer in educating and relaxing his racehorses in the hunting field and in fact took Nickel Coin out with the Surrey Union the day before she won her sixth chase at Plumpton in November 1950. The next March the O'Donoghue magic held to witness a game display when the former cripple showed her tail to a big field to win the Grand National on a diet supplemented with Guinness and eggs.

These days the twinkle is still strong in his soft Irish eyes, the talk is of simple common sense and the winners are still being sent out from the tiny yard hidden amid the bustle of busy Reigate. Jack has skillfully handled the sprinter Hello Mister to win three decent dashes in 1994 at such places as Goodwood, Newbury and Doncaster. Not only that, the tried and trusted methods that have been spawning successes for fifty years, have worked to keep Hello Mister sweet enough to race 26 times that season without loosing his zest for the game. No doubt living alongside Little Record the champion donkey and listening to the constant songs emanating from the aviary, this speed merchant thinks a racehorses lot is a pretty good life and under Jack O'Donoghue, that seems a fair assumption.

Gay Record is buried in the park adjoining the stables with a touch you would expect from his gentleman of a trainer. "Sure, we laid him in his grave in his best rugs on a bed of the finest golden straw. He did us proud and we saw him off the best we could," Jack related with the feel of a true animal lover.

The left hip is not so mobile as he would like but at 87 you have to accept that not everything will last the trip. He does not complain, nor does 86 year old Kathleen Wells who has been his secretary for 35 years, exactly the same number of Elizabeth R. personally signed Christmas cards that fill the tiny office. The current card, under glass like their predecessors, is of The Queen Mother with her 400th winner Nearco Bay high on Lambourn Downs above Nicky Henderson's stables.

This was the one that mattered as Nearco Bay jumps the last fence at Uttoxeter to become the Queen Mother's 400th winner. (Bernard Parkin).

The Queen Mother's Lunedale (Kevin Mooney) winning the Lady Godiva Novices Hurdle at Stratford in September 1983.

1974 Cheltenham Gold Cup - last fence first time round - Game Spirit (Terry Biddlecome),
Pendil (Richard Pitman), The Dikler (Ron Barry) and Captain Christie (H. Beasley).
The only one missing at this fence next time was Pendil who had been brought down 3 out.

The Argonaut (Bill Smith) winning at Cheltenham. This is how it should be done, sadly
calculations somehow go astray. (Bernard Parkin).

Proof that Prince Charles rode but never got enough chances. The only time HRH The Prince of Wales wore the colours of HM Queen Elizabeth, the Queen Mother. Upton Grey taking the third last hurdle at Newton Abbot, May 1981. (Bernard Parkin).

Bill Smith had to work hard on Sunyboy to land the Queen Mother's 300th winner at Ascot.

Insular flys a hurdle under Eamon Murphy en route to winning the William Hill Imperial Cup. (Paddock Studios).

Gerald Oxley the first leg of a Royal Treble on Special Cargo at Sandown Park despite riding the last mile without stirrups. (Paddock Studios).

Kevin Mooney partners Special Cargo (No. 10) to win the Whitbread Gold Cup with Fulke Walwyn's more fancied runner Diamond Edge under Bill Smith challenging in the red and blue colours. Bill retired after this ride.

Magic Junction schooling (the day the Queen Mother visited Nicky Henderson when the book cover photos were taken). (Bernard Parkin).

"Why so much fuss over a small race at Uttoxeter?" Nearco Bay asks his owner. (Bernard Parkin).

That picture hangs as proudly on Jack O'Donoghue's wall as the one depicting his milestone when Gay Record took his owner to the first century back in 1960.

Arthur Freeman stearing Double Star to one of his 17 victories

Chapter 7

Bill Rees:
The Gentleman Jockey

Arthur Freeman had held the Royal reins with and then after Dick Francis, gaining 22 successes on Her Majesty's horses trained at Fairlawne between March 1955 and 1960. His strongest link came with the handsome Double Star, they teamed up for 10 victories most of which were witnessed by Queen Elizabeth.

By the end of that successful partnership a young David Mould had started to make inroads as a jockey for the stable, although when it came down to appointing Freeman's successor, Major Cazalet opted for the experience of Bill Rees.

"The offer came after the Cheltenham Festival when I'd taken the Gold Cup on Pas Seul beating David on Cazalet's Lochroe, owned by Lord Mildmay's sister Helen," the quietly spoken Rees recounted. "David got the ride on the morning of the race after a nasty riding accident to Edward Cazalet who'd won two decent chases on Lochroe prior to Christmas. It turned out to be the fall to end Edward's raceriding career. He'd finished high up in the amateurs list that year but his father thought such a promising legal brain should not be subjected to further battering.

I personally thought David more than able to take the job, he'd displayed a talent far in advance of his years but the offer came to me, and after careful thought and a chat to my father-in-law Bob Turnell, whose stable I rode for at the time, a decision surfaced.

I accepted the job for three reasons, to ride the Queen Mother's horses, to have a chance to partner a greater number of winners and for the money. The retainer at the time was £750, not a fortune perhaps although 35 years ago there were not many on offer in the jumping game.

The Major called me down to Kent to see Fairlawne and to partner a few back end horses as the season tailed off. You could not fail to be impressed with the place, it was like a palace set in parkland, wonderful. The old fashioned stable yard sighted several hundred yards from the house elevated it above any other I'd seen in this country. The gallops surprised me being just a couple of furlongs up hill yet he'd proved his methods worked and indeed had topped the trainers list that year. Cazalet's 58 winners from only 25 different horses is a ratio that any modern day trainer would be pleased to attain.

The whole set up came from an age gone by, I'd been used to working breakfasts with other trainers to discuss the horses work and plan their races. At Fairlawne jockeys quickly knew their place and in the seven years I held the job I was never once asked to join the Major for breakfast. No jockey ever made the table, not even Bryan Marshall who really did command respect within racing circles.

The first time I schooled with the Queen Mother present mayhem insued. We were all circling with the horses when she appeared and as one the lads raised their caps which set the horses alight. Several whipped around depositing their riders and galloped away loose while others plunged off in diverse directions. It was quite amusing really although at the time things were fraught.

I never once heard Queen Elizabeth say anything unpleasant about any horse or human, she has a serene aura about her which certainly spreads to everyone else."

The Rip had been spotted as a foal by Queen Elizabeth in a breeding class at a Norfolk show and later in a field adjoining the Red Cat Pub in Norfolk not far from Sandringham.

The colt's owner/breeder Jack Irwin had produced him as a result of a mating his 45 Guinea mare Easy Virtue with The Queen Mother's former racehorse Manicou. On several occasions she ventured over to the Red Cat to monitor the colt's progress, eventually buying him through Captain Charles Moore, the Manager of The Royal Studs.

Jack Irwin, flattered as he was to have attracted interest from Queen Elizabeth, asked £500 for the then two year old. Captain Moore pitched it at £400 and on hearing the difference in valuation Queen Elizabeth insisted her envoy should offer 'the guineas' and the deal was done.

He like so many before him, went to Eldred Wilson's farm for his education where he earned the appraisal "Plain, ponderous and distinctly bone headed."

A spell out hunting as a four year old evoked some spark in the sloppy gelding who then joined Cazalet to be trained in the Spring of 1959. The racecourse brought him alive and in Arthur Freeman's last spell as a jockey he showed there was better to come with maturity.

The next season Bill Rees reaped the benefit winning first time out at Hurst Park. Bred and made in the stamp of a chaser The Rip quickly progressed to fences where he made his mark. He had grown into a fine big horse by the time Bill rode him to record his first success for Queen Elizabeth, a far cry from the tiny thing she had first seen the potential in.

Despite his obvious ability Rees thought the horse would benefit from the fitting of blinkers, a step rarely and reluctantly taken on the Royal horses even to this day.

The second person to suggest this avenue was Eldred Wilson who noticed the chaser hanging towards the stables with a full circuit to go at Folkestone. On this occasion Bill Rees opted to partner the useful Blue Dolphin, letting David Mould in for his first Royal win over fences.

The Queen Mother heard the news quite quickly, even though she was dining on the governor of Kenya's train near Equator station at the time. Good news carried fast via Buckingham Palace to Government house in Kenya. These days it is possible to listen in live over the telephone links.

David Mould kept the ride on The Rip scoring twice more before the stable jockey claimed his right and was reunited with the chaser to win the Cottage Rake Chase at Kempton in November of 1961. The stable could do no wrong as the Queen Mother's annual stay at Fairlawne approached. Cazalet and Rees teamed up on the first day of the month to record a four timer at Windsor setting the scene for a memorable Lingfield Park meeting eight days later. Although Cazalet ran his horses more often than many contemporaries, his mid season aim was always to produce a hatfull of fancied Royal runners at this fixture. The plan usually produced a winner or two to further boost the enjoyment of Queen Elizabeth's stay every year, 1961 proved unforgettable for all concerned.

Three Fairlawne runners on the Friday saw Out Of Town win for Queen Elizabeth under a good ride from Rees. Saturday 9th December complimented the previous day's appetiser in no uncertain fashion when of Her Majesty's four runners, The Rip, Laffy and Double Star completed the first Royal treble.

The Rip carried the extra burden of being the last to attempt the mission and as he had to give two stones of weight away to each of his rivals, appeared to have a tough task. As much as the whole steeplechasing world adores the Queen Mother, no one would dream of forfeiting victory to allow her horse to win, nor would she ever want to win that way.

Such was the case that day with both Wily Oriental and Domstar trying to sap The Rip's strength by setting a furious pace, the plot failed and the treble landed.

The Peter Biegal painting of the Lingfield Park treble, which hangs amongst The Masters in Clarence House

Peter Cazalet framed his year around this weekend and this time trumped every other occasion. Over a twenty year period The Major orchestrated the racing fun while his wife Zara matched the enjoyment by carefully creating a guest list of mainly non-racing celebrities to stimulate conversation. The recipe could not be improved upon.

To commemorate the Royal treble Honor Beckwith-Smith commissioned Peter Biegel to paint the three winning horses in various stages of preparation outside Lingfield Park's stable yard prior to leaving for home.

Double Star is rugged up and ready to be loaded up in the motor horsebox. Bill Braddon, the travelling head lad is in the process of putting the rugs on Laffy and Alec King, the Rip's groom, is washing him down with the steam still rising. Jim Fairgrieve is just checking all is well. The painting occupies pride of place among a collection of old masters in Clarence House to this day.

Of the Rip's 13 victories, Bill Rees rode him 8 times though he probably put up his best performances in defeat when third in the 1964 Hennessey Gold Cup to the mighty Arkle and even more so when making Mandarin fight all the way for a half length win at Kempton Park.

In his early association with Fairlawne, Bill managed to win three races on the French bred Jaipur who never quite had the courage to continue a successful chasing career. At the same time another Frenchman, Laffy, proved both a prolific Royal winner and a Lingfield Park course specialist adding seven other victories to his first one when part of the famous treble.

The next season after joining The Rip in doubling up at the penultimate Hurst Park meeting before the course was sold for housing, Laffy experienced a less than happy meeting with a beautiful, well dressed female.

He had been aimed at The Monaveen Chase commemorating The Queen Mother's first ever winner. It was the final days racing at Hurst Park and looked tailor made to send the course off in Royal style.

Doping scares were rife at the time and to combat such happenings five security stables had been equipped with alarmed doors and windows. Laffy spent the night before his engagement locked safely within one of these boxes and looked bright enough when Jim

Fairgrieve checked him last thing at night.

At 5.15 the next morning, Jim fed all the horses, when once again Laffy showed normal health. However by the time Jim and Peter Cazalet returned from working the horses at 9 o'clock Bill Braddon reported the chaser could hardly stand up and a panic check confirmed he was either ill or doped. The vet took blood and saliva samples which proved he'd been got at. After everyone including Jim Fairgrieve had been thoroughly interrogated by the police no internal blame was apportioned. The time of the crime was placed at between 5.15 and 5.30 a.m. during the short time the security boxes were unlocked for the morning feed.

An unidentified chauffeur driven lady had turned up unannounced a few days earlier purporting to have arranged the visit with the trainer. Not wanting to offend a potential owner or friend of his employer, Jim Fairgrieve gave the lady a guided tour of the stables. As she was never seen again and Peter Cazalet had not given anyone permission to attend in his absence, it seems logical this person was behind the doping of the Royal horse, yet to the day he died the head lad was convinced she must have enlisted help from within the stable for the administration of the drug. Fortunately, Laffy recovered quickly enough to run and win five days later at Lingfield.

It transpired the woman was the front for a gang who worked through a list of 23 stables from Kent to Scotland getting at over 40 horses.

Bill Rees remembers this horse fondly. "Laffy was a lovely little horse but he became a bit windy when the ground was at all slippery. In such conditions he would not lift off the ground at a jump preferring instead to crash into a fence.

I rode him in the Grand National, he fell at the third fence a socking great open ditch. Not satisfied with that Laffy got to his feet before me, then fell again while jumping without me in the saddle.

Before the National though, he went over to Northern Ireland for the Ulster Harp National. I was told Willie Robinson would ride the horse for political reasons. I had no say in the matter and was far from satisfied with that explanation and indeed never did manage a ride in Ireland".

The idea to run Laffy at Downpatrick stemmed from her five day visit to the province to meet a succession of duties which started with a concert at the City Hall in Belfast.

Her visit ended on the highest note having been a total success throughout. Huge crowds thronged the approach road from the town and the tiny racecourse enclosures were packed to capacity with April snow capping the mountains of Mourne in the background.

As she has always done whenever possible Queen Elizabeth drove around in an open topped Land Rover waving to and in the process, captivating the spectators affections. The motor cavalcade was flanked by George Taylor, huntsman of The County Down Staghounds, his brother Tom, huntsman to The North Down Harriers and Patrick Dobbin from The East Down Foxhounds.

On her way from the motor vehicle through the crowd even the bookies fell silent before a spontaneous cheer swept through the race-goers. One small man not on the official receiving list could not contain himself, he stepped forward and shook The Queen Mother's hand warmly.

She then met the favoured few including a line of voluntary St. John's Ambulance ladies before retiring to a glass fronted viewing box until Laffy bounded onto the course. Preferring to see every inch of the race Queen Elizabeth walked out onto the stepped grandstand to follow proceedings through binoculars.

Robinson had taken a crashing fall in the previous race and although physically fit there was some question as to his state of mind from mild concussion. Major Cazalet had misgivings when legging his jockey into the saddle but there was no one else to replace him. He had every reason to worry as to this day the only man unable to recall the race is Willie himself. Strange though it may seem, riders can go through the motions when in that state as the subconscious takes over. I am sure many of you have experienced a similar situation having driven miles, deep in thought, without actually remembering doing so.

Three of the fifteen starters fell at the very first fence with Laffy and Willie Robinson performing a neat sidestep to avoid the trouble. More of that came later as Connkeheley ran out then continued in the race prompting the commentator to state "The first horse is the second, if you see what I mean".

Robinson stayed in the middle of the field for most of the journey until Roman Folly made a break with three fences to jump. Willie sent Laffy in pursuit and once the pair hit the final steep hill in front a swarm of hats took flight accompanied by relentless cheers. Five clear lengths separated the Royal chaser from a game Roman Folly and for once the bookies paid out with genuine smiles.

Laffy strode back into the tiny winner's enclosure where his owner quickly appeared to greet him and to congratulate Willie Robinson. Turning to the crowd who had hemmed the party in Queen Elizabeth said "This has been a most wonderful day for me. Laffy and my jockey deserve full credit. They gave me a great thrill in the final furlong when storming up the hill to win."

The crowd were not going to let such an occasion finish and in the seething mass of bodies the Royal bodyguard got separated from the party. Souvenir hairs from Laffy's tail were highest on the agenda although one woman with twin daughters thought a Royal blessing for her children would be more beneficial.

Injury kept Bill Rees away from Laffy for the gelding's next two victories, although he did get back on board for a tilt at the 1964 Whitbread Gold Cup, a race in which Willie Robinson once again proved to be a thorn in his side. "I really did fancy Laffy to win this big one and all went to plan until going down the back straight this huge horse with a tiny jockey came upsides me absolutely running away. It was the great Mill House who had he been born in a different era to Arkle would have gone down as one of the all time greats. Dormant won the race but Mill House was the star.

Anyway, they ran us off our legs and in the end we finished third which thrilled the Queen Mother who is exactly the same in defeat as she is in victory, she has an amazing girlish innocence and charm.

I did manage to pick up another three races on Laffy in between regular bouts of breaking my right leg. While I was out of action David Mould and Dave Dick piloted him. Laffy loved Lingfield, which was just as well as the Major ran everything there that was sound, 8 of his 12 wins came at the Surrey course.

Another horse I found who enjoyed Lingfield was Double Star. Dick Francis had started him off with a couple of successes before Arthur Freeman struck up a partnership with the small but very useful chaser. In all Arthur scored 10 victories on Double Star. He was a great rider but was too tough on the little horse who took a violent dislike to open ditches. To combat this Arthur used to get at the horse and the harder he rode him at the ditches, the more the horse backed off the fence.

After Laffy's win in Northern Ireland, this incident at Cheltenham in 1987, when racegoer Michael Bailey broke through security and kissed the Queen Mother, proves how vulnerable she is when enjoying her sport.   *(Gerry Cranham)*

I'd seen this happening before I got the job and reasoned the opposite tactics would work. By sitting quietly with a gentle but firm hold of his head, the horse stopped fighting the rider and started to concentrate on getting over these bogey fences.

A bold leap clinches it for Bill Rees and Silver Dome at Plumpton in November 1964.

At the same time I struck a happy note with Silver Dome, pairing up to win 6 of his 7 races. He was a wild sort so we planned to give him a gentle introduction at Sandown Park where he surprised us by absolutely winning in a common canter and went from strength to strength.

Around park fences he looked brilliant yet when we ran him at Aintree he hit every single fence, how he kept himself upright I'll never know.

In complete contrast we then went to Wye, a greyhound track compared to Liverpool and we were back on the winning trail again. Bill Powell rode him to win at Kempton while I was off being plated, screwed or stretched back to health, then we agreed it was time to go back to Aintree for the Becher Chase over the National fences in October 1964.

He'd got a bit of sense by then and jumped with precision until walking through the fence before Bechers. At the time I thought he'll never get over the next yet he popped it well as if the total lapse at the previous fence had never happened.

It all went well from then on in until having jumped the last to challenge the leader Phil Harvey on Barleycroft. Phil was always a sharp operator and this day proved no different as he totally carved me up at the elbow half way up the run in putting Silver Dome into the rails. My horse had shown signs of being windy on several occasions and no one was more surprised than me to find him willing to fight back after such a crunching, when I pulled him out to go around Barleycroft, he flew.

This turned out to be Her Majesty's first ever winner at Liverpool let alone one over the national fences."

Silver Dome ran five times over the National fences;

1963/64 season
| 2nd Nov 63 | (Bill Rees) | Second | to Team Spirit in Grand Sefton Chase (left clear 2 out, weakened run in) |
| 19th Mar 64 | (Bill Rees) | Third | to Red Tide and Siracusa in Topham Trophy (led after Bechers till after 2nd last) |

1964/65 season
| 30th Oct 64 | (Bill Rees) | Won | Becher Chase (beating Barleycroft a neck) |
| 25th Mar 65 | (Peter Pickford) | Seventh | to Hopkiss (bad mistake 3rd, the chair) |

FINAL RUN
1965/66 season
| 16 Oct 65 | (Bill Powell) | ___ | Kempton Park, collapsed approaching 4th (Had heart attack and died) |

In all Bill Rees partnered 51 Royal winners and but for breaking his right leg four times would no doubt have ridden half as many again. Falls are all part and parcel of a jump jockey's life yet to hear Bill quietly reeling them off makes it seem as if there was no pain attached to the breakage's.

"Arch Point fractured my skull at Newbury. Funny thing when I got up first of all I thought I had got away with it but I was also concussed so things were a bit hazy. That kept me out for six weeks, then as is the way in racing I came back to ride five winners in a row in the space of a couple of days and went on to have a superb ride on The Rip to finish fifth in the National.

Dargent jumped as well as any horse at home yet kept falling on the track. I could not tell you why he fell in public but also I never minded riding him. Mel was different though, I told The Major I would not ride him, then poor David Mould broke his leg on him at Folkestone.

Antiar oozed class from the moment I first sat on him. We won a big hurdle race at Newcastle before he became The Queen Mother's, then Dave Dick took the Spa Hurdle at Cheltenham so it was a bit disappointing when he showed less enthusiasm for fences. That victory turned out to be The Queen Mother's first, and to date only 'Festival' win and sadly she was unable to witness it.

At Ascot, Antiar slithered and fell into the water jump where I got hung up in the stirrup iron. Luckily I managed to hang onto the reins because if he'd galloped off with my foot caught in the stirrup I'd not be here now. Some spectators held him and took the saddle off him before I could get my foot free.

Lochmore broke my thigh in the first fall after coming back from Dunkirk's tragic death in the 1965 King George at Kempton when I broke the same thigh for the first time. I'm convinced Dunkirk was dead before he hit the ground that day.

They dropped me off the stretcher when trying to duck under the rails, then I was put in traction although I'd wanted the thing pinned together. When I fell on Lochmore it transpired the leg had never healed properly. I was not at all happy and insisted on going to Swindon's Princess Margaret Hospital. To get me there they put me through the window of a train and lay me on the seat with a nurse sitting opposite in case I fell off. When we arrived at Swindon I was ferried around on a Royal mail parcel trolley but when I got to the ward it was like the Ritz.

In my absence David Mould came of age and really clicked with Major Cazalet so although I managed to ride a winner for Queen Elizabeth on Oedipe, my list of horses had shrunk and it came as no surprise to be offered £500 as a 'thank you, don't ring me, I'll phone you!' from Major Cazalet.

Bill Rees was far from ready to pack up though and continued to ride for a further six years in which time he managed to break his right leg twice more. In all he broke that leg every year for three years, had a year's grace then did it for the fourth time the next term. He points out "I think it was because the leg was stiff from the first break and used to stick up in the air when I fell after that. It appears the Jockey Club had decided to give former jockeys employment if suitable and I had been selected to become a starter along with Gerry Scott. They would not allow me to ride on to the Grand National in case I got hurt again so I decided to retire at Wincanton on Jim Joel's Arctic Beau. He won alright but when coming back through the gate off the course, dropped down dead from a ruptured spleen. What a way to go out, the girl who looked after him in floods of tears and me walking into the unsaddling enclosure with a saddle but no horse.

I've really enjoyed being a starter for the past twenty-two years, it has given me a continued link with racing and opened my eyes too. The flat jockeys don't try to help the starter. They need nurse maids, trying to get them to pay attention is like shouting at a brick wall."

Bill Rees was a beautiful horseman and a great jockey. He fitted the role as the Royal rider well, being a gentleman through and through. He has served racing without a single blemish to his name and continues to do so as a racing official. Undoubtedly a role model.

Oedipe, Bill Rees, one of the very few horses Peter Cazalet put blinkers on, but he could not overhaul Michael Scudamore on Arctic Ocean at Windsor.

Chapter 8

David Mould:
The most stylish Royal Jockey

Although he never managed to get a ride in public while serving his apprenticeship on the flat, David Mould's experience under Staff Ingham at Epsom quickly elevated him among the stable staff when weight forced him to join the jumping stable of Peter Cazalet in 1957.

Within two years of joining 'The Major', the London born son of renowned horse dealer William Angel Mould, got his chance to prove his outstanding style when riding in gallops could also prove effective in races. It did. David quickly cut his way through the army of boys who start out hoping to make it to the top and proved so good that he lost his right to claim a riding allowance in a single season.

"We had a superb bunch of horses, the Guv'nor got them ready to assault the scene from September and right through to Christmas the winners flowed. There I was, a kid from a dealing yard riding for the Queen Mother. Princess Margaret was there too when I first rode in the famous silks and I distinctly remember thinking 'Bloody Hell, what am I doing here in this company. My old Dad lived for horses but died before he ever saw me race ride. He'd have been so proud if he'd been leaning on the rails when I strode out to meet Queen Elizabeth.

I never had any doubts about being able to ride as I'd been brought up to stick on anything and everything that Dad bought and I can tell you there were some rough ones among them.

Our yard was in Ashford in Middlesex which is part of London now but then it was open countryside. I hardly ever went to school as more often then not Dad would have some wayward beast that needed educating more urgently than I did.

So there I am standing in the parade ring at Kempton Park sporting the Royal colours as bold as can be. It was not a swollen head, more a case of knowing that if the horse was good enough it would get all the help it needed from me.

Chaou II clears a Kempton Park fence in 1971 under David Mould

Most lads going out for their early career rides have had relatively little experience of making horses do what the rider wanted them to do. Racehorses usually exercise in Indian file and are rarely asked to vary the routine, the same goes for young riders.

My education at home came on horses whose main intention seemed to be channelled into ridding themselves of the nuisance on their back.

From that very first introduction Queen Elizabeth put me at ease straight away and I found chatting to her a relaxed situation. I still pop in whenever I'm passing Clarence House. The Queen Mother loves to hear the gossip although these days she appears to be more in touch with what is happening than I do.

Racing's littered with fairy tale beginnings or endings and this inaugural ride on Queen Elizabeth's King Of The Isle became another of them, he gave me a winner at the first attempt."

Right from the outset David Mould stood apart from the crowd for his smart dress sense and to the practiced military Cazalet mind that suggested the newcomer would also take pride in his job and horses. Without knowing it, Mould had leapt several rungs on the ladder even before his natural ability in the saddle had become evident.

"It was because I had nothing, I looked after what was on my back. The others sniggered at me for pressing my jodhpurs every evening ready for the next day. My boots shone like a mirror and I'd iron my cords for evening stables. What I had, I looked after.

From the age of 17 Fairlawne was my home and my life, it was everything to me until the Guv'nor died in 1973. The discipline could not have been stricter, it was certainly a hard school yet we all knew the score and no quarter was given nor asked for. Everyone had their job to do and was expected to do it properly. We even had a tack man to clean the saddles and bridles, we never cleaned our own tack.

The yard was ruled by the clock. When it struck 6 a.m. we were expected to be in the stableyard and at 1 p.m. we could go to lunch. We worked in the evenings from 4 to 6 p.m. when the horses were fed and only then could we go back upstairs. Those sort of hours take some getting used to for young lads straight from school."

At the time when David Mould started to catch the trainers eye, the quietly spoken Bill Rees held the position as stable jockey and so he naturally had the pick of Cazalet's three runners in Folkestone's long established Fremlin's Elephant Chase in April of 1961.

At the time Mould was perfectly happy to ride The Queen Mother's The Rip, rejected by Rees in favour of the same owner's Double Star.

"I'd never sat on the horse 'til the Guv'nor legged me up in the parade ring and that's where all those years of being chucked up on all sorts with Dad, paid off. I'd learned to evaluate a horse before he got my measure and so by the time we'd reached the start I knew The Rip had heart for his job.

This was the horse the Queen Mother found herself in a field behind a Norfolk pub, she loved him all the more for the extra bond they shared. His thirteen wins and a good third in the Hennessy more than vindicated her judgement.

I loved the horse too, he had guts and was as tough as old boots and somehow we just felt good together. He was a great big horse, yet as gentle as could be. He really was the original Gentle Giant. When he was turned out in a huge paddock and I'd call his name, he'd come over to be fussed. Most horses like attention although some will never respond while others accept it, but the odd one like The Rip give you back as much love as you give them.

It's a bit like two really good human friends, even when they've been parted for a long period they slip straight back into the relationship.

As we won the Folkestone race I kept the ride for the next season winning The Grand Sefton Trial at Hurst Park and a good chase at Newbury before the Mould Christmas jinx struck again. I spent the first four Christmases as a jockey in hospital. The initial time I got injured it was no more than annoying to miss the big Boxing Day program of races, then as the pattern became monotonously regular with me forced to watch other riders winning on my horses, it went beyond a joke."

After his fourth Royal winner when The Rip strolled home at Newbury on November 9th 1961, David had to wait another five years before he again partnered his old favourite to the chaser's final victory at the hilly tight Plumpton course in October of 1966.

In fact it was to be two years before he even rode another Royal winner due to injury and illness.

"I'm long and skinny and snapped when I hit the deck hard. In the early 60's we only had thin cork shells to protect the head. They had no chin straps which meant when you were flung out of the saddle your helmet left your head long before you hit the ground. Another factor and this is not just an old jockey talking, the fences were honestly a lot tougher then. Up at Manchester they would not give an inch, any error had to be paid for with horse and rider rolling in the wet grass, I hated riding there.

The only consolation about being hospitalised after Christmas was that the old man had bagged three quarters of his season's tally by then. I never once completed a full season without some sort of breakage. I've done twelve collar bones in my time, in the end they got fed up so I had a steel one put in. My skull got fractured, a broken pelvis and quite a few splintered ribs stopped my gallop. Oh and my right leg snapped four times. I'm a bit like a matchstick.

Our horses were schooled superbly, twice a week they all went through a jumping session and our fences did not give a single inch. Not everyone felt such a need to teach horses to negotiate obstacles at speed and too many horses I rode for other trainers had little or no steering, brakes or manners. One horse frightened me to death at Folkestone by refusing to turn into the back straight. Without any fuss or fighting it simply ignored my attempt to persuade it to negotiate the right handed bend, preferring to gallop directly towards the outside running rail and crash through to the car park without even ever checking it's stride once.

As I'd been leading the pack for the first half circuit Richard Muddle, who now owns Wolverhampton and Southwell racecourses, boldly followed me through the railings assuming I knew where I was going!!

When our horses were fit they worked for their corn. The old man believed in running them and often horses would be on the course twice a week. It certainly paid off but unless we were forced to shut up shop by bad weather, they had all gone over the top by the Cheltenham Festival.

Most of the older trainers used to insist on their horses being out at exercise for at least up to two hours, the Guv'nor's had done their work in twenty minutes and were back in their stables long before other trainer's horses had warmed up. It worked for us then as the same method did for the legendary Tom Dreaper in Ireland. Now, thirty five years later they're all at the same game only now it is done on all weather gallops.

A few incidents will paint a picture of the regime for you. The Major saw a cigarette end lying in the yard and demanded the culprit to own up. As it had not been any of us, no one stepped forward so he sacked the lot of us, yes the complete staff got their cards. It turned out that the postman had dropped the offending object and we were reinstated.

Another time he walked into the yard to see a boy standing on a low wall with his hands in his pockets, asked him what his wages were and promptly told him to go to the office, collect his £2.10 and get off the estate at once. The boy could not believe his luck as he skipped down the drive, he had only come to deliver some meat from the local Butchers shop! He didn't even work for us.

You will appreciate, I did not know the old man any better the day he died than I did the day I joined him 26 years earlier. He only once invited me into the house in all those years and only then because Marion had come to the yard with me. It was a real 'tug your forelock job', yet we were devoted to him.

Game Spirit and David Mould, Newbury 12th, February 1972. This is Queen Elizabeth's favourite picture of the horse   *(Bernard Parkin)*

I got the leg up on Super Fox who although basically a second division horse, managed to win three times at The Queen Mum's favourite course at Sandown Park. At the same time one of the best and gamest horses the Queen Mother ever owned joined the stable, he was a French import called Makaldar and he became my hero.

If he was running now with the rules the way they are, he'd have a job to win purely because he was so idle I had to bully him from start to finish, he needed stoking for every inch of the way and these days I'd have used up my quota of slaps in the first mile.

Makaldar never had an easy race in his life, I used to jump out of the gate and smack his backside all the way and he kept digging deeper.

He was such a kind horse though, he'd forgive me anything, he never turned sour or once looked around at me. On the odd occasion when I'd got to the bottom of a horse, the clever ones would look back at me as if to say 'look, I've given all I've got. What more do you want.'

I had to knock spots off him to win and that is the one thing that Queen Elizabeth would not tolerate, she hated her horses being hit. Most times after I'd ridden Makaldar the old man would say, 'She couldn't watch you know'.

I'd see her afterwards to explain that Makaldar was so lazy he would not race at all if I did not keep at him. She'd reply 'Yes, I do understand', and then she'd look at his quarters to see if I'd marked him but he never did show any signs of the hiding he'd had."

Makaldar won six of his seven outings as a juvenile hurdler in 1963/4 including Haydock's Victor Ludorum. On that occasion David had thought there would not be sufficient pace on for Makaldar's stamina to come into play so he asked flat jockey Brian Taylor to make it a proper race on a horse of Ken Cundell's. It is not uncommon these days for a rider of an unfancied runner to force the pace as a favour or even for monetary consideration.

"The plan looked flawed at half way as a flat race gallop is several notches up from a decent jumping pace and Brian went so quick I thought he'd gone off his trolley. Anyway, Makaldar jumped so brilliantly it kept him in touch until the blistering pace burned the opposition off to let us cruise home in the end."

David Mould was forced to miss his next three victories through injury, successes at Sandown Park and Newbury twice let Bill Rees back in for further Royal winners.

David got back on board a year later when they took a modest Folkestone hurdle as a warm up for the Mackeson Hurdle at Cheltenham's November meeting, winning both.

The tough chestnut won again at the Gloucestershire course the following season after almost a year off with leg trouble. Major Cazalet then used Newbury's March meeting to sharpen him up only a week before the Champion Hurdle, a ploy few of his colleagues would dare risk. It is just as easy to overcook the roast as it is to leave it underdone.

"It should have worked too", David reflected. "It turned out to be my biggest disapointment. At the last jump in the 1967 Champion Hurdle Saucy Kit ridden by Roy Edwards led Aurelius, who'd won the St. Leger before proving unsuitable for stallion work, with Makaldar under hard driving from me joining the issue and definitely reeling them in. Being such a tough nut, I knew he'd keep pulling a bit out up that final thrust to the finish, I really did think we'd win.

I could not believe what then happened to me. In those days the Gold Cup start was situated where the tented village is now leaving a wide expanse of track at a tangent to the finishing straight acting as a lure to any horse with wayward tendencies. Aurelius saw it, ducked across the course taking Makaldar with him, allowing Saucy Kit to go for the prize unchallenged.

When that sort of thing happens there are no signals, one minute you're driving up the hill for all you're worth and a split second later we're almost doing a U-turn and heading for the Malvern Hills.

After a shouting and barging match with Aurelius we both reversed our flight, headed back on track and continued to battle it out for second place with no hope of catching Saucy Kit. We finished third, then were promoted to second at the inevitable Stewards inquiry and subsequent disqualification of Aurelius.

The form book may tell you we would not have won even with a clear run but I knew this horse better than anyone and his ability to keep pulling a bit more out up the hill would have got him there. Queen Elizabeth has only had one Cheltenham Festival winner, there have been some hard luck stories on the way but few unluckier than Makaldar. I realise the Queen Mother had more dramatic reversals than this one but as with Devon Loch's National, she took this defeat on the chin. The reaction was always the same, win, loose or even if I'd ridden a bad race, she's just the greatest, a lady through and through."

The huge angular chestnut with ears like a donkey was an extraordinary shaped horse. He carried little flesh on his big raw boned frame yet his heart must have been twice the size of most of his rivals.

He only won two steeplechases, the first of them the prestigious 'Black and White' Gold Cup at Ascot in November of 1967, although his biggest fan did not particularly want to ride him in the race.

"The old sod would get so close he used to walk up the guard rails over fences before taking off. He'd part a jump half way up and in those days the fences took few prisoners. I can honestly say he frightened the life out of me. We ran three horses in the race although I tried my hardest to persuade the old man not to run Makaldar as Three No Trumps owned by Prince Rajsing of Rajpipla looked a certainty. I realised I had to ride my old buddy if he ran so the obvious plot was to get him re-routed elsewhere, it didn't work.

At the start I looked over at Josh Gifford on Three No Trumps thinking he could well win while I might end up rolling in the dirt. What people fail to grasp is that even when a rider thinks he will not win a race, it does not prevent him from doing his best, we're all out there to win and when the Blue and Buff silks are on your back there is an added incentive.

They went a fair pace with Makaldar struggling from the gate. I'd been knocking spots off him just to keep in the race and when we reached Swinley Bottom I thought what am I doing this for but he kept making steady progress on the leaders.

On the run to the last fence we only had Pat Taaffe in front of us and we inched past him to win an exhausting battle. You cannot imagine how fatigued a fit jockey can be at the end of a prolonged struggle. The truth is, horse and jockey were so knackered when the old boy stumbled on the cut up ground after passing the finish, I went straight over his ears like a complete novice. He galloped off for a lap of honour finding new reserves from somewhere while I sat in the grass trying to get some breath back."

His old legs gave him trouble again keeping Makaldar off the course for a little over two years when he managed one further success in the Londesborough Chase at Sandown Park to give David Mould his thirteenth victory on the horse he admired most for his courage and willingness. Three No Trumps the horse the Royal rider had wanted to partner instead at Ascot became the property of Queen Elizabeth and a year later Mould teamed up to win on the handsome gelding to win at Sandown.

Peter Cazalet kept himself in the best company yet never minded dropping his horses into the worst if the move looked fruitful. When skipping through his winning partners David evaluated Ballykine as "Not very good but well placed by the Guv'nor to win four races within five weeks. Ours were not wrapped in cotton wool, they had to work for their keep."

Ballykine started his winning streak over hurdles at Folkestone at the end of September then took a second victory at Wye and within a couple of weeks added two novice chases around the tricky Sandown Park fences.

"I hated Wye, it resembled a dog track. Even so, the place proved lucky for me. If you got out of the gate fast no one could get past you as it was almost round, a bump here and a nudge there saw off all-comers. I was top jockey there for years but still hated the place."

Around this time Bill Powell got his chance, although he was always going to be up against it to make the break. Bill Rees and I had the bulk of the rides between us with David Nicholson creeping in for the odd mount. Willie stood taller than me and suffered from a stutter which made him withdraw into himself. The Guv'nor tried everything he could to help Willie get on including sending him off for elocution lessons. He could ride well enough and did get two Royal winners on Silver Dome and Mel. The latter came in the horse's first novice chase at Birmingham and having done the dirty work, Willie lost the ride to Bill Rees two weeks later when that pair took the Channel Tunnel Chase at Folkestone. You see they were plugging the thing thirty years ago, we never thought it would happen."

Mel had been sired by the Queen Mother's Manicou who'd taken the King George VI Chase in 1950 under Bryan Marshall. The only other two winners Manicou sired for Queen Elizabeth were The Rip and Isle of Man. There were twelve years between this pair who both proved streets better than Mel.

Bill Powell was the only jockey they could not trace when it came to the 400th winners party in October 1994, he has disappeared without trace.

Another of the successful French breds to boost both Cazalet and Mould's tally came in 1969 in the shape of Chaou II and his appearance also heralded another prolific winning rider in Richard Dennard.

Chaou II won five races over hurdles and fences under David in his first season at Fairlawne, the pair notched fourteen successes in all with Dennard stepping in for a further three victories.

"Now he did do the business in some style," David recalls "He came to us as an almost black grey with strong dapples and like me he had turned white by the end."

Queen Elizabeth went to see her horses at Fairlawne often though early December each year saw a long and special weekend of racing, watching schooling sessions and gallops complimented by well balanced parties. She felt so relaxed within the confines of Fairlawne that often when keeping himself fit in the Park, David would come across The Queen Mother walking alone.

"I'd always ask if I could talk to her and she'd say 'Oh yes, do walk with me and tell me all that is happening on the racecourse'. She is far more knowledgeable about horses than you'd imagine. Not just breeding or what they'd done but the little things that only real officianados would pick up.

If a horse looked a bit dry in its coat or had lost weight on its quarters, she'd pick it up. Also, despite the old man being restrained when she was around, she knew his traits. She often said 'He is such a fierce disciplinarian, isn't he?' and I'd smile and nod.

The Queen Mother loved to be a hands on owner, she always made a fuss of her horses, patting and talking directly to all of them in turn. We invariably paraded her string around her in the park which at one time numbered 25. Once after The Rip had won the day before at Lingfield, she held him for a photograph to be taken with Jim Fairgrieves waving his hat in the air to make the horse prick his ears. It had the desired effect o.k. as The Rip took fright and pulled Queen Elizabeth clean off her feet!

Queen Elizabeth as a child on her favourite pony, Bobs

You can imagine the panic as she refused to let him loose. She held on to him as he dragged her bodily across the grass and she just refused to give in to him. Everyone shouted 'let go, let go' but she held on until he stopped. Then before any of us could reach her, The Queen Mother got to her feet and said in that lovely voice, 'Well, now I know what it's like to be a jump jockey!' The most amazing thing about that incident is that she was 64 years old at the time."

The Queen Mother had ridden from a very young age and indeed used to try to keep up with her elders on an old donkey, who had obvious ideas of his own, the merest sniff of water sent him plunging into the burn with a shrieking Elizabeth on his back. She had better rides though when intoduced to her favourite pony Bobs.

"Schooling proved a bit hairy as there were inevitably loose horses running around the park. The Major would be biting his lip while he muttered to the fallen rider to catch the thing.

I was a stubborn man and could play him a tune too. He had a go at me one day about a bad race I'd ridden and would not let it drop. All the way back to the stables he roared at me until we got to the gate and said 'Well, what have you got to say then?' When I replied, 'Pardon Sir? I didn't hear a thing you said', it threw him into a rage. I was teasing the boss and he knew it.

The incident almost ended our relationship. I'd mistaken the winning post at Sandown Park and stopped riding only to get beaten by an old screw we'd thrown out two years earlier. The Guv'nor convinced himself I'd stopped the horse, Three No Trumps, for the bookies and reported me to the stewards. In fact he dragged me into the inquiry room making such a row that they ejected him to interrogate me.

It looked worse each time they replayed the film. The truth of the matter was I could not see out of my right eye for half of that season but had kept quiet about it. I knew he'd stop me riding if he got to hear the proper reason so I insisted I'd actually mistaken the winning post and as there were two, ten yards apart, they accepted my explanation.

The Guv'nor however did not. He ordered me to report to his office the next morning after second ride, leaving me with the threat of standing me down for a month. Not only would that have been costly in lost earnings and winners, other trainers would have believed me to be crooked. I had to out-fox the fox.

I'd bought a house at Epsom for £400 and kept my savings under the bed there. I gathered the £2000 he'd paid me as a retainer, stuffed it in my pocket and marched boldly into the office taking the offensive to him.

'Here's your money. I've had enough. If you can't trust me there is no future for either of us. I'm off.'

The Major used to whack the desk with his military cane, all the lads were outside earwigging the outcome. He looked me straight in the eye and then at the pile of readies at which point I turned and walked to the door praying to God he'd call me back.

It took until I'd got my hand on the door handle before he coughed and said 'Em David', he never ever called me by my Christian name so I knew I'd played the right hand, 'Come on back, we've both said silly things, let's forget it, shake hands and forget the whole thing.'

Not another word was ever said on the subject, he was a man to respect and I adored him.

Fairlawne is a mansion and usually there were plenty of guests staying at weekends. Fulke Walwyn came down a lot but was never allowed into the stables. Every time Fulke asked to see the horses he met a brick wall which only served to convince him that the Guv'nor had a second yard. For ages he'd quizzed me about the existence of one as we regularly produced eighty winners from thirty to forty horses and Fulke refused to believe it possible.

David Mould, the winning most Royal jockey on Chaou II at Sandown Park in 1975. *(Gerry Cranham)*

Just as I had edged Bill Rees out, Richard Dennard made inroads on my patch eventually being able to claim a percentage of the rides as his own. He first rode a Royal winner on Chaou II, crept in for Retz and Woodman, got a few on Escalus, Newborough and Zaloba but with Inch Arran and Black Magic, he really came of age. He was never going to wrestle the job from me but, as it happened, the two outstanding horses of 1970 and 71 were Richard's rides.

I only rode Inch Arran once when Richard had an injury. The grey chaser was a wild horse, he fell five times and won fourteen races. I'd never even sat on Inch Arran's back prior to doing so in the parade ring before the Topham Trophy at Liverpool and then I very nearly failed to get there in time.

David Mould urges Inch Arran over the last at Aintree to beat Philip Blacker (now a famous sculptor) on Quintus, in the renowned Edward Courage colours.

My brother Wally had driven me north and while I slept in the back of the car he gaily carried on up the A1 heading for Newcastle instead of going over the Pennines from Yorkshire to Lancashire. The Guv'nor had stayed at home to watch the race on television with Queen Elizabeth. He was dying of cancer although none of us knew it at the time.

Our head man Jim Fairgreave called the shots and, even as the time ticked by towards the deadline for weighing out prior to the race, he steadfastly refused to let Lord Oaksey pass the scales even though he was dressed in The Queen Mother's colours and mad keen to have a crack.

We arrived with only minutes to spare and then the gateman tried to stop us from driving anywhere near the stands so I jumped out leaving Wally to sort it out and ran up to Oaksey who was forcibly stripped of the Royal colours as I pulled on my breeches and boots.

Inch Arran gave me such a confident feel as he attacked the first fence I knew then he'd take all the beating and he duly sailed around the huge fences to win well. I loved riding over the National fences as it demanded skill and in return left a tingle for ages."

Another outstanding chaser Mould excelled on when winning eleven races in the space of two years came in the shape of Game Spirit. He took two hurdles before being put to fences where his jumping made racegoers gasp in admiration. It was after Game Spirit's eleventh victory that Peter Cazalet died and the decision made by his son Edward to close the stables and end Fairlawne's steeplechasing history on a high.

"The old horse was a Gent, most beautifully balanced, oozing class and probably the only racehorse I rode that could have gone to the top as a show jumper. When the place closed down and we all made our different arrangements, I chose to ride for Newmarket trainer Tom Jones and actually asked the Queen Mother if she would send Game Spirit there for me to ride.

The request failed for political reasons as Tom had not long been divorced and at that time it did not curry favour. Twenty years later Tom's son, Tim became one of the Queen Mother's trainers when Jim Joel died and left her the choice of his horses. She chose Keep Talking who was in training with Tim at the time.

The horses all moved to Fulke's at Lambourn and he rightly decided that it would not be fair on his jockeys to miss out on the Royal dozen. Although I did get one ride from his stable for the Queen Mother, my era as Royal jockey had run it's course with 106 winners in the Blue and Buff silks. I feel very privileged to have been there during such an exciting period in racing's history. I never once wished bad luck on my former rides when watching them run with another jockey in their saddles but I did often think, Lord how I wish it were me up there."

I hope it has come across from the tales within this book exactly how much The Queen Mother enjoys the company of her racing friends. She has captured everyone's heart because not only does she epitomise everyone's idea of the old fashioned meaning of the word 'Gay' but she loves life to the full whenever the opportunity presents itself.

David Mould still has a cosy bond with Queen Elizabeth, cemented not only by his century of winners for her but also from the injuries he has sustained while trying to win her another first prize.

"When I'd got a plaster cast on my right leg from ankle to thigh, it coincided with a party for The Queen Mother's 150th winner. I did not want to go to attract attention away from the healthy jockeys only she insisted I join the fun.

It meant sliting the leg of my dress suit trousers and putting a zip in to cover the plaster and as I drove an old Ford Zodiac with a bench seat, I could jam my straight leg onto the accelerator, slide across to the middle of the seat and steer the car, knocking the rigid leg off when needing to slow down. It proved a challenge right enough and you should have seen the doorman's face when I levered myself out.

Queen Elizabeth said 'How good of you to come David, I've got a stool for you to rest your foot on during dinner and hope you will dance with me afterwards? You'll be fine'.

We had several dances and she kept saying 'This is wonderful'. I replied 'Have I knocked into you yet?' and she said she'd tell me when I did. She wanted to know all the inside gossip from the weighing room but seemed concerned if I told her there had been some raised tempers.

Even as recently as 1990 which is 16 years since I last rode for her, The Queen Mother showed genuine interest in what is happening. Marion gave birth to our son Jack in a London Hospital at 2.30 a.m. and when she had settled down I wandered outside to take it all in, only to find myself passing Clarence House at 6.30.

Knowing someone is always on duty I called in to leave the news, only to be asked in by Sir Martin Gilliat. There I sat, unshaven and looking like an exhausted tramp, toasting Marion and Jack with champagne."

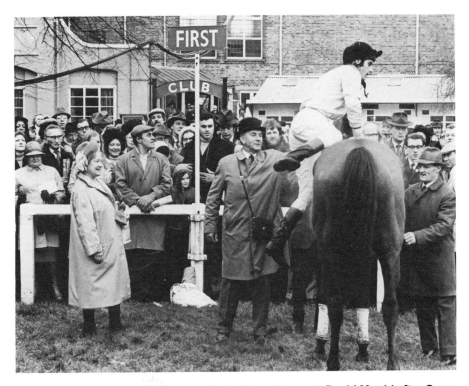

Just months before he died, trainer Peter Cazalet greets David Mould after Game Spirit wins The Royal Windsor Handicap Chase in January 1973
(Gerry Cranham)

When David retired he helped Marion in her role as international showjumper, loving every minute of the involvement. He'd done it as a kid and could appreciate the ability and commitment she so obviously had. The man who had been in the driving seat for twenty years happily moved over to navigate for his wife. "Marion is the most wonderful horsewoman, I just got sheer joy from watching her. She was very strong at the time and didn't want to do anything else. I loved her, still do very much. I just did the best I could for her".

David, Marion and five year old Jack Mould live in Lymington, the south coast yachting town near the New Forest. Jack is a natural horseman who regards his gift at this stage as less useful than being able to kick a football well. In racing we breed the best with the best hoping to get the best and in the Moulds' case the legend looks to have worked a treat.

Chapter 9

Richard Dennard:
The end of an era

Richard Dennard never worked anywhere else than at Fairlawne which made the end of that era even harder for him than most.

A Dover lad, Dennard first tasted the life at Fairlawne when on a fort-night's trial during the 1959 Easter holidays. He took to the grandiose surroundings and both Peter Cazalet and Jim Fairgrieve agreed the boy would fit in there. The stable's strict, almost military way of doing things would not suit everyone but Richard being neat and tidy himself felt he would blend in.

He joined full time in September that same year having left school at fifteen. "Short back and sides hair cut, polished boots, clean working clothes, always wear a cloth cap, no ear rings, nose studs, smoking or facial hair, address the boss as Sir and never be late, were the ground rules." He smiled on recollection, "From the age of eight I'd known I would become a jockey although it turned out to be a long haul. There were several good lads there at the same time all looking to make the grade, even John Cook who later won the Grand National on Specify never managed to get a ride from The Major while he worked for him. John held the position as head man in The Bothy where we lived above the stables, that was a fun place when work ended for the day.

It was definitely a hard station ruled by the clock tower. If someone failed to make it into the yard as the clock struck he lost his half day off that week which in any case only amounted to two hours off in the evening.

Even though their was no room for error, we held the Guv'nor in the highest regard as he radiated honesty and a sense of duty. Even those lads who could not stand the strict regime came back after finding easier jobs less satisfying.

You can imagine when I first held a horse for The Queen Mother to inspect I was agog, then as the visits became more regular she put me at my ease, a gift she has with everyone. It amazed me in my early days there The Queen Mother would mention it if a horse had changed stables since her last visit. She knew the ins and outs of the yard as well as any of us who worked there.

It amused me to watch the Guv'nor trying to move her along when she wanted to talk to someone that he considered could embarrass him. Old Bunny Dunn the blacksmith swore like a trooper and treated every person exactly the same. Queen Elizabeth used to make a point of going into the forge to see Bunny without fail and loved his earthy stories.

The forge would be spotless along with every other potentially mucky place, even the manure lorry's strawy trail disappeared under a flurry of yard brooms the moment it pulled away. The sight of a cigarette butt in the stable area prompted a mass interrogation under sentence of instant dismissal.

The whole regime moulded us into better people and would not go amiss these days when important values have gone out of the window, we were proud to be part of Fairlawne."

Richard Dennard ironically sustained his worst injury in a motorbike accident at the end of his first year, returning fully twelve months later to continue as a groom with his hopes still pinned on the stable jockey spot. At the time Arthur Freeman held that position then Bill Rees took over with David Mould always that little bit ahead of Richard in the pecking order.

He progressed to being second in command to Jim Fairgrieve in breaking in the young horses and finally got a chance to ride schooling. When entrusted to take the Queen Mother's latest French purchases, Retz and Chaou II, up to Clarence House for the owner to see what she had bought, Chaou II reared up and broke loose. The grey galloped all over the lawns and flower beds with a sweating Dennard in vain pursuit. The only person not perturbed was The Queen Mother who watched with amusement as Chaou II gave her a show that no one had bargained for.

After sticking to the mundane duties for the first five years, the chance to ride David Mould's rejected novice chasers on the course provided the opening he knew would come one day.

"My first ride for Queen Elizabeth came on Woodman at Folkestone, just a few miles from my home at Dover. The Queen Mother could not make it that day but just to walk out to the parade ring in her silks was the proudest emotion. All my old school mates and family turned out to cheer me on, when we won they enveloped the winners enclosure, it was magic.

She did attend though when I next rode him a year later at Newton Abbot where he slipped up and was so badly injured he had to be put down. We all were in floods of tears when I met her afterwards but she is strong for everyone despite what she feels inside, saying 'We've come a long way and will do so again, this is the down side of racing but we must put it behind us.'

I had attained the start I desperately wanted but had to still look after two horses during evening stables at that time, one of which was Escalus. I led him up when David Mould won on him at Folkestone, then only four days later swopped the lead rope for the reins riding him to win at Sandown Park. Now that is a thrill, to ride a horse you look after at home gives a jockey an extra special bond.

Inch Arran came home on his own 4 times in a row but Richard Dennard never lost faith or his bottle. *(Bernard Parkin)*

Richard Dennard and Inch Arran became a formidable partnership. At Kempton Park in 1972, beating Richard Pitman on New Romney   *(Gerry Cranham)*

Things started to accelerate for me then as I had horses that were designated as my rides not David's cast-offs, although the first of them did come to me because he was a bit over excitable. At that time we did not know the Queen of the Isle family, they all turned out to be lunatics with ability. The first one to join us was Inch Arran.

You had to ride him at exercise on his own as he boiled over in company and would plunge off regardless of where he headed and that is scary. The answer was to give him as much rein as he wanted, once you caught hold of him, he'd lose all reason. On the racecourse we could never bring him into the middle of the parade ring as he would have taken the stewards and The Queen Mother with him. Instead I vaulted into the saddle as he paraded behind the others and once on board exited quickly before he realised what was happening.

Mouldy must have thought what a clever boy he'd been stearing clear of this one as Inch Arran proceeded to fall in each of his first four races!!

Inch Arran's trouble stemmed from his natural boisterousness, he picked up so far in front of his jumps it looked impossible for him to clear them and sometimes he didn't.

His fifth outing came at no less a place than Sandown Park where the fences invariably win any arguments resulting from a horse failing to respect them. The morning before the papers indicated 17 horses had been left in so it looked assured of being a fair old cavalry charge after the final declaration deadline later that day.

Before this date with destiny I had been booked to ride at Nottingham. I managed to get buried in a chase and remember laying in the grass thinking at least I won't be fit to ride that crazy Inch Arran the next day. Luckily, before I told the Guv'nor I would not be fit, a pressman bounced up to me to get my reaction to having a walkover on Inch Arran the next day. Walkover! I could not believe my luck.

When this happens you just have to canter down to the last fence, turn around and canter back past the judge. I do not think it could be linked but ever after that easy day out he clicked and started winning. He was my ride earned through following orders just as Major Cazalet's men would have followed him in the war.

When we won the Winterbourne Chase at Newbury to record our 9th success beating other good horses I came in off the course with a grin like a Cheshire cat only to be swiftly put in my place by the Guv'nor who had Queen Elizabeth beside him, 'You can take that stupid grin off your face too Dennard' he barked. 'You kept looking over your shoulder. I won't have it, look where your going not where you've come from!' Mrs Cazalet and Queen Elizabeth were laughing about it at the 400th winner party at Ascot in October 1994 and that was 23 years after the incident.

David Evatt experienced Inch Arran's special thrill in a race confined to amateurs and then David Mould got the call at Aintree when I'd broken a collar bone."

Zara Cazalet remembers that win vividly, being the last her husband Peter trained for Queen Elizabeth before he died. "Peter had been unwell for eighteen months but wanted to share this race over the National fences with his owner and dearest friend. They lunched at Clarence House and watched David Mould conjure some breathtaking leaps from Inch Arran who provided them with the perfect finale to a marvellous partnership. The telephone sounded almost instantly to which Queen Elizabeth said 'That will be The Queen' and it was, she said 'Well done Mummy, well done'."

Dennard nursing his broken collar bone continues the story, "In all the old horse provided eleven of the thirty seven winners I managed in the Royal colours.

Black Magic arrived with the same outlook on life too, only he proved even faster over the first three fences than Inch Arran. This one also scrapped me off his saddle several times in the early days of the partnership because he looked more intent on fighting me than looking where he was going.

This chap came a size bigger and that bit stronger, he really only stayed a mile and a half but went so far clear of his rivals by the time he folded up, nothing could get back to him even though he slowed dramatically near the finish. Thrill, adrenaline surge, you name it, he gave it to me in some style.

At the starts I had to stand him sideways onto the starter as the second I turned him towards the tapes he exploded into action. At Sandown he often jumped the second fence as the others toiled over the first!

With two such madcaps to ride during the same period Queen Elizabeth felt acutely aware of the situation and would always say,

Few horses got this close to the bold front running Black Magic and Richard Dennard. (leading Australian Champion, Chaser Crisp and Richard Pitman)

In the 1960's jockey's never flinched at racing through water logged ground and all for £7.00 a time.

'How do you feel Richard? Black Magic must be the most thrilling but also terrifying ride. Please be careful and have a good ride if you can.' That about summed it up, the line between excitement and fear is quite thin.

Most of ours had gone over the top by the Cheltenham Festival, yet I'm convinced Black Magic was good enough to take the Two Mile Champion Chase if only the second fence had not upended us.

Another horse that became my ride due to circumstances was Master Daniel. At the time both David and myself were trying like mad to ride The Queen Mother's 200th winner and as it came to the beginning of December 1969 it looked sure to happen. David lost his temper during a race at Folkestone when he thought the amateur Peter Upson had deliberately cut him up and retaliated by landing a blow with his whip across Peter's back. The stewards saw the incident, gave him three days suspension and in doing so handed the ride on Master Daniel to me. We recorded the second century of Royal winners at Worcester on the 3rd December 1969 and because we'd clicked I retained the ride.

This landmark gave The Queen Mother a good excuse to throw a party at The Savoy for everyone connected with the winners and it is one I shall never forget as she asked me to dance with her, that is something I will always cherish.

Breakfast of egg and bacon was served at 3.15 a.m. to draw the dreamlike event reluctantly to a close.

I can't tell you how The Queen Mother makes people relax in her company, she does it without you realising what has happened. My wife Diane first met her at Edward Cazalet's wedding. We were living in a caravan at the time and Queen Elizabeth easily kept the conversation going for twenty minutes on the rigours of caravan dwelling. She is just so genuinely interested in people's lives.

When the Guv'nor died in 1973 The Queen Mother had agreed to visit a university in Scotland. The fact she came down to Fairlawne proved what regard she held for the place, the staff and the whole racing diversion. We were all called individually into the Stables office where she quietly reminisced over the common areas of whatever our job had been. Everyone from the jockeys to the gallop man was received and presented with a personalised memento ranging from cigarette boxes through travelling clocks to cuff links all inscribed with her crest and initials. 'It is all so sad, Fairlawne has been a second home to me for a long time, racing will never be the same. I'll continue of course and will enjoy watching the horses do their best but how can such complete surroundings be replaced?' She was so right, Fairlawne provided a world in itself, we were self sufficient and only needed to venture away when racing.

I'd been very fortunate with injuries, apart from the leg broken on the motorbike I only broke collar bones, wrists and a shoulder blade plus one concussion from the horses.

Having talked things over with Diane, moving to other stables seemed uninspiring after the fourteen years I'd been at Fairlawne. Edward offered the stables to me to carry on a livery business but Jim Fairgrieve would still be there and that could have been uncomfortable so I became a painter and decorator with the Fairlawne Estate houses a regular provider of work.

Ten years of that, even with four men working for me, lost it's appeal. We bought a shop and flat in Norwich City centre, worked our hands raw and now thirteen years later sell the finest porcelain and wooden artifacts imported direct from Italy where we seek out and select the items personally.

On reflection I'm glad we did not have the money or backing to train, racing can make people rather insular and it would have been hard to match let alone better the life we'd enjoyed at Fairlawne."

Most of the staff felt the same way including head lad Jim Fairgrieve who wrote of his employer, "The Guv'nor was a perfectionist, anything he did however unimportant, had to be absolutely right. He was a strict man, and could not bear incompetence. He was quick to anger and equally quick to forgive. A great humanitarian, no one ever had a raw deal from Peter Cazalet. To do something stupid and admit it was forgivable, covering it up was not.

He did not like Yes men but if an opinion was different to his it had to be substantiated. He gave permission for any request but hated being taken for granted. Carelessness, incompetence and dithering he abhorred, even a dripping tap would be mended at once.

He had a wonderful sense of humour while believing there was a time and a place for it. He was not a back slapping man and his aloofness was often misconstrued. He was my idea of a real man, honest, upright, Godfearing, courteous and kind when it was merited, outspoken to say the least when he was annoyed. I think my poem speaks for everyone who was employed by him at the end."

The sound of the stable is silent
Now the horses have all gone away,
The sun may be high in the heavens
But the cloud over Fairlawne is grey.
No more will the dawn be awakened
By the whinny of impatient steeds
as I open the door of the feed house
and give them their first morning feed.
No more will the sound of their hoofbeats
Resound through the fog in the park,
No more will we go to the race meets -
The future looks gloomy and dark.
So lock up the door of the stable,
Start walking, never look back.
Bite your lip just as hard as you're able,
If you don't, then you're quite sure to crack.

The Queen Mother always has a smile for everyone.   *(Gerry Cranham)*

Peter Cazalet and subsequently Fairlawne were no more but for everyone else, life had to go on and it did, but to a man those closest to the heart of the story fiercely guarded their own special memories, allowing me to only scratch the surface in these pages.

Chapter 10

Moving On: Fulke & Cath Walwyn

When Peter Cazalet died Queen Elizabeth had two dozen horses to decide what to do with, causing much hopeful speculation among not only trainers who'd enjoyed previous social occasions in her company but also from jockeys hoping to be in a position to wear the Blue and Buff silks.

As it turned out Michael Oswald approached Fulke at Epsom on Derby Day to enquire casually if the Lambourn trainer had room for twelve horses. "Yes" he could accommodate that number, the yard had no inmates at the time as they were all out to grass for the summer recess and such an offer should be investigated further. The two men would meet up again the following day at Epsom before the first race.

Cath Walwyn, who had been every bit of 50% of the training partnership, heard the news from her husband the first evening, "Strangest thing happened today", Fulke mused. "Some chap asked me to take a dozen horses though he did not actually say they were his, he looked familiar though I can't quite place him."

After a description Cath lit onto the identity and the plot unfolded. They had been asked to train for the sport's most high profile owner and Fulke's weathered face assumed an even ruddier glow.

Cath Walwyn recalls "We'd been to stay at Fairlawne on many occasions and had been in Queen Elizabeth's company when she stayed

Royal Trainer, Fulke Walwyn   *(Bernard Parkin)*

with my brother in law, Derek Parker-Bowles. Even so we had not thought our chances of being honoured with the string very bright. There was a strong rumour at the time that the Queen Mother would give up her racing as things would not be the same without poor Peter Cazalet and the whole Fairlawne thing.

It is quite funny really to look back as at that time, Dave Dick who'd won the 1956 National on E.S.B. at Devon Loch's expense, came to ask us one day if we had been approached as there was betting on who would be the next Royal trainer.

Dave pressed us hard but Fulke stuck to his story and as he left us Dave headed off to have a huge bet on Fred Winter."

I can testify as stable jockey to Fred, the Walwyn's closest neighbour, that we had hoped to at least share Her Majesty's string. Amid our own disappointment we did agree that we were pleased for the team 'over the wall'. Beside Fulke, Jack O'Donoghue took charge of Colonello who went on to win for him at Sandown under Charlie Goldsworthy, while the popular Borders trainer Ken Oliver handled Earl's Castle and later Burning Bush, winning with both chasers.

Nick Gaselee who later trained for Prince Charles had the unenviable task of going to Fairlawne to collect the Queen Mother's main string in his capacity of assistant to Fulke Walwyn. It was a day of mixed emotions for Nick who had been brought up only ten minutes away from Fairlawne and had ridden a winner on Queen Elizabeth's Oedipe when outriding Ben Hanbury.

"I used to ride out for Peter Cazalet in the days of The Suez Canal crisis when there was petrol rationing. My transport then was my point to pointer, Kinrosshire. Everyday I'd ride him over to Fairlawne, leave him in a stable while I exercised two lots for Peter then canter back home on my old chap.

You can imagine how sad it was for those left at Fairlawne to watch as we loaded the last dozen horses into motor horse transporters. Having seen the stable at it's height and then to be emptying the stars, made me want to join Jim Fairgrieve in tears. Conversely the nearer we got to Lambourn, the more excited I became at the thought of being involved with handling the Queen Mother's horses.

The Royal dozen arrived at Saxon House in July amid great excitement from trainer and staff. As each horse trooped from the transporters, blinking at the summer sunshine and whinnying like school children on the first day of a new term, the Saxon House team drooled at the thought of the winners amongst them. Game Spirit, Inch Arran and Isle of Man were the stars.

Fulke trained in a very different way to Peter Cazalet whose methods had been governed by his estate's layout. In the park he only sent the horses two and a half furlongs uphill, as that is the longest strip of suitable land there. He would do that two or three times which is what everyone is doing now only then it was necessity, now it is choice.

As we had the hundreds of acres of the Lambourn gallops and our own land behind the stables, we adopted a more traditional method. Lots and lots of roadwork to harden them off turning summer fat into winter muscle, followed by endless long steady cantering.

It also took 25 minutes to get to the gallops from our yard which meant they'd done a fair bit of work simply to get up there and he firmly believed in walking back very slowly to cool off and let the muscles relax naturally. Now with the dominance of interval training up and down all weather strips the horses are only out of there stables for half an hour.

Our's used to be out for three times that length and as a result we could only ever have two lots per morning. Now they seem to be in and out like yo-yos and the evening grooming session when trainers traditionally looked at each horse has mainly died out too.

We thought that was as important as the morning work. You could see how each horse had benefited from his exertions or if his legs showed signs of strain. Fulke had a knack with legs and although we had our share of tendon trouble, many strained tendons were saved by him feeling trouble before the naked eye could detect it."

Of the two that excited us most at Saxon House, Game Spirit became the first to win for the new owner/trainer partnership at Newbury on the 23rd November 1973 under Aly Branford. On Boxing day a month later, Isle Of Man doubled the score at Kempton Park with Terry Biddlecombe in the saddle.

That day's feature chase, The King George VI went to the spring heeled Pendil who was to be involved in many battles with Walwyn's chasers.

Three days later back at Newbury, Terry steered Game Spirit into the winner's enclosure and within a week Isle of Man and Tammuz provided Walwyn's first Royal double at Sandown Park for the blond curly headed rider.

Game Spirit continued to add a further two good chases to the rising total then Terry rode the proud horse into third place behind Captain Christy in an unforgettable Gold Cup at Cheltenham. My mount Pendil went off the odds on favourite only to be brought down at the third last fence when still pulling my arms out to let him go for home.

There had been a telephonic threat reputedly from the I.R.A. to shoot the horse if he looked like winning. When I recounted this fact in the changing room after the race, Biddlecombe released my own tension by putting the matter into perspective. "Jeez Pitters, I was besides you all the way, they might have missed and shot me instead." Then he roared off to ride in the next race.

That day saw the people's hero go out for the last time when he partnered Amarind in the Cathcart Chase, then the final race of the Cheltenham Festival.

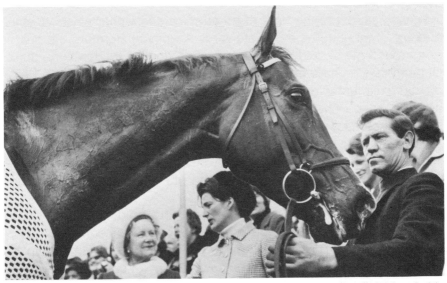

Game Spirit, one of The Queen Mother's favourite horses after finishing 3rd in the Cheltenham Gold Cup. *(Bernard Parkin)*

I again rode in this contest and was absent mindedly totting up the Festival earnings, having won the Champion Hurdle on Lanzarote, when we reached the course. Belatedly realising this was Terrys moment I pulled back to let him canter off first and will never forget the wall of noise that greeted his emergence.

The Cheltenham public gave him a send off that had never been heard of before nor since. You had to have been there to appreciate the volume of spontaneous cheering which must have equalled the noise the Aintree crowd emmited when Devon Loch looked the assured winner of the1956 Grand National.

Although holding every chance of a dream goodbye for most of the race Terry's horse cried enough between the last two fences and my mount Soothsayer went on to win. British racing has always been the straightest in the world and not only would it have been totally wrong to let Terry win, he would not have wanted to go out on a winner as a result of charity. He'd proved himself and held his position at the top through ability.

Terry had a boyish charm that oozed from him so naturally that Kings or paupers would enjoy his company. If that was not enough for one man he could also inspire horses to give their best with or without much persuasion.

Having almost robbed me of an early career winner when weaving a web of total untruths at the stewards enquiry at Hereford, he put his arm around my shoulder and said "it was worth a try don't you think? Hope there's no hard feelings but learn from today, talk as good a race as you have just ridden!" How could you have any animosity for such a tousle haired character and he received just the same admiration from his horses.

The seeds had been well and truly sown for the successes to come, 115 for Fulke and a further 7 for Cath after her husband's death in 1991.

It fell upon one of the home breds, the bold, jockey frightner, Colonius to get Fulke off the mark the second season in a novice chase at Warwick on 24th November 1974 under Bill Smith. In the space of the next three years the chestnut won 13 chases to add to his hurdle win for Peter Cazalet.

Colonius did his owner/breeder proud even if his apparent self destruct ideas at the fences did little for her blood pressure.

Colonius only ever won in the first and last few months of the season when he could hear his hooves rattle on the firm ground. His annual holiday came during the dankest part of the year when the big guns were firing but in terms of carrying his workload towards the owner's total of successes, Colonius sits high on the list.

Cath recalls "About the same time when things were rather touchy, Fulke almost broke a blood vessel himself from temper. He used to often wander about the stables out of working hours, watching and listening for those small but vitally important sights and sounds that tell an experienced person if all is not right.

A horse may be scraping the stable floor with a front hoof - 'Could it be the onset of colic? Is that a cough coming from the end stable? If so then get it moved now, not in the morning when the infection will have had ten hours to spread. Is that horse almost breaking out in a sweat on this cold evening? Take its temperature!'

He must have seen something odd and as he pulled the stable door to, the outside catch dropped down, imprisoning him with Isle of Man who as bad luck would have it, would kick you if he could not bite you.

The stable was one of the inside cage boxes off a passageway in the stone barn. As the name implies the door had bars above the normal half door level and Fulke became imprisoned with the meanest horse we had. Well, he shouted and roared for all he was worth risking more damage to his health than the horse who evidently thought he would be the cat and Fulke the mouse.

After he had been gone an hour it did occur to me that he had taken much longer than normal, then Liz our secretary came to the house saying strange noises were coming out of the barn. Strange noises hardly did justice to Fulke's language when we did let him out and when we told the Queen Mother she roared with laughter at the thought.

Among the first group of horses we had, Colman won at Towcester, Present Arms at Sandown, Just Lit at Warwick and of far more importance Sunyboy at Ascot and Wolverhampton.

It could not have gone better for cementing the relationship as in November of 1974 we produced nine winners for the owner to watch having just come south after her annual holiday in Scotland.

The middle to late 70's saw a steady flow of successes from the stalwarts. Game Spirit actually had the speed to finish second in the Two Mile Champion Chase in 1976 having been placed in the Gold Cup two years before over an extra mile and a quarter.

Isle of Man also ran placed in the Two Mile Champion, we got so close to achieving a win at The Festival, yet not quite.

Sunyboy who was a full horse kept things going when his Ascot win in the Fernbank Hurdle made it 300 winners in 1976 for the Queen Mother, followed by the home breds Queen's College and Upton Grey.

The latter won twice for us and also became the only mount Prince Charles had in his grandmother's colours. He was not really suitable as he had limited ability both galloping and jumping.

The Prince came down to acquaint himself with the grey in the early days of his courtship with Princess Diana. The press knew his every move and they swept over the place like an oil slick until Fulke saw them off with his walking stick and some earthy country language."

"I don't much like my prospects," Prince Charles could be saying, when walking the course at Newton Abbot, prior to riding the Queen Mother's, Upton Grey.

Prince Charles rode well enough and at the time was riding out regularly for Nick Gaselee who had a couple of horses for him.

Basically the horse could not have won when Prince Charles rode him at Newton Abbot as the going had got too soft but the engagement suited his diary. Nick Gaselee accompanied the Prince to Newton Abbot and remembers the day well. "It had not been a good year for

Prince Charles, his best chaser Alibar had been killed and the replacement did not prove suitable. This amateur riders' hurdle at Newton Abbot looked ideal but the ground became soft which he hated. Anyway, after much discussion we decided to go. Upton Grey went a mile and a half then Prince Charles wisely pulled him up. He said he enjoyed the day, the banter in the changing room and the friendliness of it all. He adores polo and hunting and would not have followed racing to the same extent as the Queen Mother or Princess Anne.

I remember him saying half the people expected him to do well because they assumed he'd be on the best horse while the other half think it's quite funny if he fell off. He knew he would not please everyone whatever happened."

Tommy Turley, Fulke's man in charge of the horses when they went racing, thought Prince Charles rode the gelding as well as any pro could have done that day. "He went around the inside rail where the brave men go and could not have got another ounce out of the horse. Upton Grey could not win in that heavy going.

If he was disappointed it did not show but regardless of the result he gave me a tenner 'to buy a drink with'. My wife Anne said I should have it framed as one day he will be King of England. I said no, Prince Charles wanted me to have a drink on him and I did."

When I made contact with Prince Charles regarding that race he said it was one of the proudest moments of his life to ride in his Grandmother's colours on Upton Grey even though he wasn't placed on that very wet, muddy day.

Cath Walwyn takes up the story again. "Princess Anne came down to school here too when trying a horse that we thought would make an eventer. Mark Phillips schooled it first and was not at all keen for his wife to do so but she insisted and loved it. She came out tops in our book although at the time was not thinking of raceriding.

The way Fulke and our vet continued to patch up old Special Cargo and Tammuz's legs never ceased to amaze people.

There are so many little things that continually need decisions and one almost caused us the most embarrassing situation. Special Cargo's Whitbread was to be his last race that season, very nearly ours too as it happened.

He had this strange deficiency within his system after being in training for six months every year. His coat dropped out in large unsightly patches, he almost became bald in a blotchy way. He looked so odd we considered not running up to a week before the race.

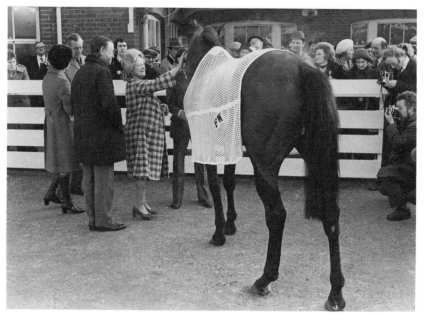

Fulke Walwyn rightly looks pleased after producing the bad legged Tammuz to win the valuable Schweppes Gold Trophy at Newbury in 1973. *(Gerry Cranham)*

Fulke came up with the bright idea to cover the bald spots with black shoe polish but took the precaution to ask the vet Bobby McEwen if it could seep through to the blood system and be considered as an illegal substance. He assured us it would not.

Special Cargo looked amazingly well and even though the polish liquified during the race, in the winners enclosure it was impossible to spot the cover up, he sweated so much. The Queen Mother must have known when she saw the state of her gloves after giving him a victory pat but nothing was said.

A week later the Jockey Club notified us that the samples taken in the dope test afterwards were not totally clear. Well Fulke went absolutely bananas at poor Bobby who had to sheepishly admit if the horse sweated enough the bootpolish and Indian ink could be absorbed through the pores.

There was little sleep in this house for the next week and the lads kept out of the boss's way without knowing the pressure he was under.

The second sample proved clear and we all breathed again. Imagine having won the Whitbread through sheer bravery in the last stride only to loose it later through a tin of Cherry Blossom shoe polish and some Indian ink?

That race must rate as one of the most thrilling in living memory, four horses locked together with the naked eye unable to separate three of them. At the time I did think we were first and second but in which order, Special Cargo or Diamond Edge, I could not even guess. Amazingly, only one of those first four horses home ever raced again in public, they could never have bettered that day anyway.

Special Cargo broke down although we managed to patch him up to win another two Grand Military Gold Cups. Racing in soldiers races is not half the workload that competing in top open class company and the old chap enjoyed his work. Horses in training are looked after like royalty whether they are owned by a Queen or the village blacksmith.

He'd already won the first of his three Military Gold Cups the year he took the Whitbread, each time with our assistant Gerald Oxley in the saddle albeit on one occasion, only just.

In 1984 Gerald came to us from his regiment in Germany for a two month stint with a view to shaping him up and if possible, to find a ride for him in the Cup.

There is a lot of rivalry among regiments and since the steady decline of numbers in the armed forces, the choice of rider for a suitable horse has shrunk considerably.

By the time the race entries were due to close it became obvious we had nothing for Gerald to ride in the race and as it is gaulling to be young fit and healthy yet forced to watch contempories from the loneliness of the grandstand, we dispatched him back to Germany.

The very next morning over breakfast I suggested asking The Queen Mother if she would permit Special Cargo to run in it and when she reacted with enthusiasm we phoned Gerald's Colonel and, red faced, asked if he could return. He sat in our house drinking a gin and tonic that very same evening and a week later won the Cup for the first of a record four times."

The last of those victories in 1986 saw Gerald at his most brilliant if not stylish when one leg of the Queen Mother's treble, Gerald produced the most extraordinary exhibition of race riding having suffered a broken stirrup leather at the 19th fence. "I was a bit worried about the next fence because I kicked the other foot free of the stirrup too, but once I cleared another fence successfully I stopped worrying. Special Cargo had a marvellous front on him, is really well balanced and jumps brilliantly so it was not too difficult to to stay on board", the squeaky voiced rider modestly recalled.

Once again the continuing familiar lines cropped up as it was Eldred Wilson's horse Prydell that Special Cargo beat, ridden by John Sunnocks from the Blues and Royals and recommended to him by the Walwyns.

Tommy Turley filled in more of the details. "Gerald brought this ancient saddle to the yard that his father had used for donkeys years. The Guv'nor took the precaution of making him take it to the saddlers to have it overhauled. They added new straps to it and passed it fit but one stirrup leather gave way under the strain. They were the old pigskin type that stretch for years on end, for this one it broke at a crucial time. The old man went mad at Gerald, he never blamed anyone when horses broke down as that could not be avoided but this could have been foreseen and costly. Queen Elizabeth has won four Military Gold Cups which has been done twice before. She badly wants to make it five which will be difficult to equal."

Tommy recognises the Queen Mother's kindness to all stable staff as she invariably shrugs off her trainers, manager, Lady in Waiting and detective to make contact with the lads. Not only is she being polite but enjoys hearing the stories that perhaps her trainer has not thought necessary to divulge. Most important though as far as they are concerned, she looks them straight in the eye and talks to them as one human to another and sadly that is not always the case with horse owners.

Queen Elizabeth also includes stable staff at her racing functions. "One year when an invitation came for me and Anne to attend a dinner at Clarence House, it coincided with our holiday at Butlins Minehead camp. We had breakfast at Butlins and dinner with the Queen Mother and much to our kids annoyance no one believed them when they said where we'd gone!" Tommy laughed.

Cath Walwyn is also quick to point out how natural Queen Elizabeth is with everyone. "She accidently knocked over a glass of gin and Dubonnet after watching some horses schooling one Monday morning and while we were rushing about looking for a cloth the Queen Mother got down on her knees to mop the stain up with some tissues. The next Sunday one of the tabloids ran the story stating 'The Queen Mother scrubbed the stain with all the vigour of a Yorkshire housewife cleaning the front door step on her hands and knees at the age of 83'.

She happened to be down again the day after the story had appeared and when I showed the story to her she roared with laughter. Quite coincidentaly, half an hour later when she was using her arms to demonstrate a point another drink went flying. Quick as a flash Queen Elizabeth was on her knees again saying 'Well if the papers say I do the mopping up, I really should' and she literally did it again.

On two occasions we benefited from a lead by Queen Elizabeth's car. Coming out of Chepstow on a Bank Holiday having our last runner in the final race, Fulke happened to say we would have a long queue at the Severn Toll Bridge and would never get home. We were told to tuck in close behind the Royal car and sure enough the passage across the crowded bridge opened up like Moses at the Red Sea.

After Tammuz won the Schweppes Gold Trophy the sponsors asked us all to lunch at their Marble Arch headquarters. We went to Clarence House for drinks first and I accompanied the Queen Mother in the car with Fulke following in ours. The Chauffeur drove us straight through The Queen's gate into Hyde Park which is something that only the Royal family can do and poor Fulke had to go around the traffic island like everyone else. It was a wonderful thing to do and so often since I have driven past the arch and remembered that time when we went shooting through it.

They only managed to get Fulke up to Sandringham once for the annual Kings Lynn Festival, he did not change his habits often. 'Culture festival', he grunted, 'What's that? Chamber music I suppose. Well that's not my idea of a weekend's fun.' Anyway we got him to go and sat him on a gold chair for three hours, lightening the day by touring the Royal studs.

That came ten years into the partnership and during that time the Queen Mother came down a lot as Lambourn is only three quarters of an hour from Windsor. She usually visited on a Monday as there were less engagements early in the week. Everyone looked forward to these mornings because she is so very knowledgeable about horses and she possesses such a good memory for the smallest details. Everyone loves Queen Elizabeth, not for who she is but because she is so genuinely friendly to the grooms. Besides talking freely she never failed to bring up something personal to each, if not about the horses they looked after it would be some family matter. Two lads had joined us with their horses from Peter Cazalet's days, forging a link with that happy chapter in her life."

The Queen Mother always chats to stable staff and enjoys their tales.
(Gerry Cranham)

Cath Walwyn drove her husband to race meetings and did the leg work when horses had been put to them for sale. To bolster the numbers that had dwindled from a high of 25 with Cazalet to half that, Desert Wind, Sunyboy and Special Cargo were purchased while Rhyme Royal joined the Queen Mother from her daughter's string.

1980 did not set any Royal records alight yet it prompted Jack Logan of The Sporting life to write, "Owner of the Year, the Queen Mother for the joy she radiates, the example she sets and for being her. Trainer of the Year, Fulke Walwyn, for walking with Queens nor losing the common touch and maintaining an astonishing record of consistency in turning out winners."

On both accounts he echoed the thoughts of racegoers everywhere.

When the Queen Mother reached her 80th Birthday the Jockey Club decided to mark the occasion with the present of a horse and gave us the job of selecting it. Ron Barry who rode for us then suggested a horse called Master Andrew would fit the bill and on paper it seemed right.

The horse had not raced until five years of age then ran a promising sixth of 28 runners at the now defunct Stockton course at odds of 14/1. Next time backed down to 6/4 favourite, he landed the gamble at Wolverhampton with a claiming jockey Neale Doughty in the saddle.

In his final race that first season the promising youngster could only finish third at Catterick when odds on to win again. Far from disgraced in the 23 runner field, trainer Gordon Richards wrapped the horse up with thoughts of what was to come.

On Ron Barry's advice the horse joined the Walwyns and although he did win three novice hurdles in his first season for them, only managed one chase win the following term.

Master Andrew had a mind of his own and when he did not want to go away from the yard would become as stubborn as a mule. The job of riding this exasperating horse at home fell to Ricky Pusey who became the fittest lad in Lambourn once he found the key. Ricky would run beside Master Andrew all the way to the gallops occasionally vaulting into the saddle only to have to revert to running as his unwilling mount dug his toes in again. Once on the top of the downs the cunning gelding would work quite contentedly on the home gallop as like a pigeon he knew it headed beck the way they'd come.

He acted the same on the racecourse, often giving away 200 yards at the start then moodily condescend to join in the race. In view of that spoilt behaviour it is a wonder the Walwyns and Bill Smith graced the winners enclosure four times with this one.

When it became evident the horse would not do anything he did not want to do, The Queen Mother gave her permission to put him 'on the box'. This inexplicable method of diagnosing and also treating ailments through a series of magnetic fields housed thirty miles away from where the horse was stabled, using a hair from the patients main or tail, worked a treat. Master Andrew became a nice guy, the down

Mark Bradstock one of the 3 jockeys to partner the Argonaut to his 15 successes. "Was I right to give up a job in Insurance for this? Yes, Yes, Yes." *(Paddock Studios)*

side was when he was good at the start he never became involved in the finish. When he behaved like a sheep, he ran like one.

The bold Ricky Pusey had his reward for the endless miles he trotted along side his wayward home partner when winning in the Royal colours on Russhill in a novice chase at Ludlow. Somehow, I do not think too many riders envied him at the time.

Mark Bradstock who was assistant then, remembers Master Andrew causing another problem. "In the stable he could be difficult around his hind legs and one evening when we took his temperature, via his rectum, he lashed out causing us to jump clear letting go off the thermometer. Horses naturally clamp their tails down when anything alien is around that area and sure enough Master Andrew imprisoned the glass phial.

On lifting the horse's tail to resume proceedings to our dismay the thermometer had totally disappeared inside him. The vet Bobby McEwen got the job of trying to retrieve it and knowing the horses ability with his hooves made several futile approaches. By then Master Andrew had become fed up with the game and really kicked at Bobby with such ferocity he farted the thermometer out like a missile. In retrospect that was the safest way for man and beast."

Mark had joined Walwyn after spending three years with the family insurance business which had seen him studying in France, Spain and South America. His parents bought him a horse to ride in races which Fulke trained to win four times in his first season. Such a heady introduction made working in the City pale into insignificance and Bradstock never did return to his day job. Two years as a lad, one as pupil assistant and five as assistant trainer provided the embryo trainer with a thorough grounding.

"Having an amateur's license and being qualified for the military races due to an eight week training stint at Pirbright, it was pure Hell. I dropped in for the ride on The Argonaut in several army races, including one which made me part of an incredible day at Sandown when Queen Elizabeth had her third and most recent treble.

Insular won The William Hill Imperial Cup, Special Cargo took his third consecutive Horse and Hound Military Gold Cup and then The Argonaut swept me to victory in Dick McCreery Chase. That was a serious thrill, being the last of the treble the crowd started to roar us home long before the final fence. That sort of verbal encouragement does actually lift your game and just as I thought it could be possible I heard that Tim Thomson Jones thundering up behind me but I managed to find reserves I did not know I had and have never found again.

The Argonaut becomes the 3rd leg of a Queen Mother treble at Sandown Park in December 1986.   (Gerry Cranham)

Quite amazingly, I then kept the ride against professionals once as Queen Elizabeth liked the way I rode without using my whip. The truth is I had a job to keep balanced with two hands on the reins let alone take one off to give a horse a smack, still it got me three winners on horses owned by The Queen Mother for which I shall be eternally grateful.

I had the utmost respect for Mr Walwyn, he won with some of the slowest horses in training and what tunes he played on old broken down fiddles never ceased to surprise me. He also managed to save one decent bet for himself every year, usually on a horse that none of the rest of us thought had a chance. He could see when a moderate beast had changed long before it became evident on the gallops.

Fulke's was a fun place to work where occasionally we could turn the tables on the boss if he'd been in a prolonged bad mood. One horse needed to have the top of his stable door wired up to an electric current to stop it biting the door to suck in air, a practice that soon destroys their respiratory system. Obviously it would be turned off during evening stables but now and again we'd leave it switched on and wait for the Guv'nor to lean on it as he looked at the horse. Juvenile? Maybe but very satisfying when we'd had a hard time."

"You know, our sport is hard with such long hours that people in other jobs could not conceive anyone doing it and yet when things go right the satisfaction makes all the worry disappear", Cath Walwyn sighed. "Sindebele had the ability to win the Champion Hurdle only he broke a leg and was destroyed at Cheltenham after just one solitary victory.

Fulke had the flu and was at home when I phoned to tell him of the tragedy and as fate sometimes decides, we lost another horse at the same hurdle the next day. Those type of happenings take a lot of getting over as we and The Queen Mother come to think of them as family.

Fulke Walwyn's travelling head lad, Tommy Turley, gives The Queen Mother the benefit of his inside knowledge of her horses.

The Queen Mother joins Bill Smith and Fulke Walwyn in celebrations at Sandown Park after Isle of Man becomes the jockey's 500th winner.

The first foal sired by Sunyboy then came into training. She arrived as a five year old having been leased from Christopher Sweeting who had bought the stallion when his racing career ended the day he became Queen Elizabeth's 300th winner. Sunyone did win though she lacked any real ability. Even so it was nice to train Sunyboy's first off-spring.

A much better Sunyboy joined us called Sun Rising. He won six first prizes mainly in the hands of Kevin Mooney who took over when Bill Smith retired.

Kevin had come to us after serving his apprenticeship with Barry Hills on the flat. He worked his way up to stable jockey and being a naturally quiet person, never fired the public or press's imagination.

Special Cargo's Whitbread was the only win Kevin had on the old horse but it was the one which mattered.

There were odd winners in the last few years like Yes Master, Dudley, the horses that resulted from a fertility experiment in Newmarket and First Romance, who is now the broodmare Queen Elizabeth is pinning her hopes on for that elusive Gold Cup winner. As with so many of hers, this was well named, First Romance is by the stallion Royalty out of the mare Roman Meeting.

I certainly enjoyed the few years I trained after Fulke's death, then due to the dwindling numbers and rising costs it became unviable. It is a young man's game now, you have to go night clubbing to attract new owners these days and I think that is not quite my scene."

Chapter 11

Bill Smith:
From Moss Bros. to Royal
Jockey

London born Bill Smith has racehorse owner and long time successful tipster John Blake to thank for his eventual career in the
saddle, of which, despite winning bigger races, he notes riding The
Queen Mother's Tammuz to win the important Schweppes Hurdle at
Newbury and partnering her 300th winner on Sunyboy at Ascot as his
most precious moments.

Always smartly dressed from a young age, Bill worked for the
famous clothes hirers as a means to support himself while he figured
a way to break into the fascinating world of steeplechasing. His break
came when answering an advert in the Chichester evening paper in
1968.

John Blake had long owned a selection of racehorses trained by the
ex-fighter pilot and war hero, Bill Marshall. Like numerous others
before him he got bitten by racing's magnetism and decided to double
the pleasure by training a couple himself. Oh yes, the pleasure
doubles right enough and with it the strain.

Bill got the job of riding out at ten shillings a morning, the fact he proved to be the only applicant having a great deal to do with the decision. John's wife Julia rode out with him for the first four days as John was away, she reported the youngster to be polite, neatly dressed and could ride far better than the average amateur who turns up looking to be another Lester Piggott.

Keen to test the capabilities of his hired help John Blake put Bill on Silver Meade, 'a huge nutty mare' and smiled at what he saw, a natural horseman and for the equivalent of 50p a morning!!

"Bill drove an old van that he'd paid £8 for with a shaggy haired Alsatian dog to guard it. He's done well since and now drives a huge Merc and Range Rover and a host of Alsatians to protect his home and stables. He was a certainty to succeed."

John Blake gave the casual labourer his chance and Bill delivered the goods at the first time of asking after two educational outings, the gamble was landed, the tipster's clients were happy and the jockey was on his way. Who could have foretold the smartly dressed young jockey in the £8 van would go on to ride 51 winners for the matriarch of one Royal family then retire to be bloodstock adviser and confidante of another, the ruling family of Dubai.

Blake's former trainer, Bill Marshall, quickly cottoned on to Smith's potential and within four days he had a ride for one of the shrewdest horse handlers in the U.K. This union worked for both parties and the dapper Smith vividly remembers those first lessons. "Bill called me up to the owners/trainers bar afterwards. Growled at me 'Do you back horses and are you honest?' when I said no and yes in that order, he replied. 'Good, now F.. off out of here and never let me catch you drinking on the racecourse again!'

Another early instruction on the finer art of making one horse go faster then another came after I had marked his horse with my whip in a desperate finish when the money was on to win. In the heat of the moment I'd hit the horse down the ribs missing the diagonal stroke across the hind quarters. Bill exploded when he saw the marks and punched me in the stomach before explaining, 'See how you like being hit in the midriff, it just creases you up. Now watch what happens when I kick your backside, you'll go out of here like a scalded cat. The correct way to use the whip is the same.' As gruff as he appeared, Bill Marshall was an animal lover and quite sentimental although casual observers would need binoculars to see it."

Smith's career took off with an ever increasing circle of trainers using him, including Fred Rimell for whom Bill partnered Comedy of Errors to win the Champion Hurdle in 1973.

The year prior to that he got the call to don the Blue and Buff colours of Queen Elizabeth on the Jack O'Donoghue trained Colonia at Ascot in the race before he was booked to partner the leading steeplechaser of the time, Spanish Steps.

"I could not have been happier," he smiles. "To ride in the Royal colours and have a big chance of landing the feature race too. Wages and prestige!

In the parade ring The Queen Mother repeatedly told me 'Do please be careful, she's not a very good jumper. Look after yourself and both come back safely, remember you have a good ride in the next race.' Well that was enough for me to make every effort to keep my skin intact and after several dodgy jumps I decided to please the owner, pulled the mare up and trotted back safely. By rights I should have offered her the riding fee back." Next time out at Fontwell Park, spurred on by guilt and pride when asked to ride Colonia again, Bill Smith gave his all to finish a gallant second, the best placing possible on form.

The jockey then had his turn on the sidelines through an unusual accident cantering down to the start on Les Kennard's Lotus Land at Devon and Exeter racecourse.

The rider relives the moment. "The horse had no brakes or steering and had a tendency to do the unexpected. He ducked out at a hoarding displaying the ironic message 'WELCOME TO DEVON & EXETER', my knee smashed into a hundred pieces and the only welcome I got came from the pain killers in Exeter Hospital!!"

Bill Marshall heard of the smash, rushed to see the patient and promptly removed him the 210 miles to the London Clinic of Tucker and Thomas in Park Lane saying, "If the little bastard's got no money, send me the account." They saved the leg although it hangs at an odd angle twenty two years later.

There is no incentive to return to work more powerful or effective, than the thought of someone else riding your horse. The chance to partner Comedy of Errors in the 1973 Champion Hurdle proved the best medicine. The pair triumphed by one and a half lengths and two lengths over Big Ron Barry on Easby Abbey and Bobby Beasley on Captain Christy.

The following year back at Cheltenham, Bill got the chance to defend his title on Comedy and started at odds of 4/6. As it happened I beat him on Lord Howard de Walden's Lanzarote which proved to be another nail in his coffin as retained rider to the Rimells.

Chatting only recently Bill destroyed a long held belief as I thought it was one of the few occasions that I'd won a race through superior tactics and punch. The defeated jockey put me straight when recounting Terry Biddlecome had told him the horse was not right before the race started. Oh well, at least I'd felt smug for 20 years. Racing has a habit of elation replacing despair and a month later at the same venue, Bill rode a much classier steed in the Royal colours, Inch Arran already the winner of 13 races for Queen Elizabeth and one of the inmates of both Peter Cazalet and Fulke Walwyn's stable.

"You need a bit of luck in this game and I'm sure Queen Elizabeth had gone to church twice that morning because we got the luck of ten people." Bill explains, "The old boy had seen his best but had made the running for much of the way then had no answer as several horses swept passed us. In situations like this when a winning chance has gone, I used to relax, enjoy the ride home and try not to ask my mount silly questions at the remaining five jumps.

At the top of the hill we were fourth of the six horses left standing. One pulled up lame then the Grand National third, Eyecatcher, fell at the next leaving me a distant second assured of collecting the £190 for the Queen Mother when I could not believe my eyes seeing the clear leader Henry Morgan's tail flick up into the air high above his back telling me he was falling.

I would be a liar if I told you I was unhappy to see the abrupt removal of the sure winner. Luck goes around in circles and this was our turn to get the slice with cream on it. Memories are short in racing though no one could begrudge the Queen Mother such a gift after what she had so graciously accepted in 1956 at Aintree."

That proved to be Fulke Walwyn's only Royal winner that season but it was enough for him to offer Bill the job of replacing Terry

Biddlecombe who had lost the battle with his weight and retired. It was felt the same route should be followed for Inch Arran who went hunting during his pension years.

The 1974/5 season started well for the new partnership as Colonius preferred the early term firm ground and set the ball rolling. "Fulke was a gentleman who had seen a few fools come and go and so wasted no time on pleasantries. He could be gruff but was fair. Until the winners started to go in every year it was best to keep out of his way and not try to make idle chatter. I got my first proper rocket from him over Colonius, Fulke launched into me, he just went mad for no reason that I could fathom out. I could not have been more surprised if he'd slapped me around the face with a kipper. Until the winners came he could be very unreasonable, it was nerves really.

Colonius obliged in September at Warwick which settled all our nerves although he'd certainly stretched mine in the race. He terrified me at the obstacles, preferring to see how low he could hit a jump without actually falling, luckily for me the rains came, forcing the front running lunatic to be put on ice until the ground again firmed up in the spring when he added two further victories to the score."

It was hardly surprising Bill viewed dodgy jumpers with suspicion as he soon experienced the second serious breakage to both his shoulder and pelvis on the aptly named SHATTERED for Newmarket trainer David Ringer, which let Aly Branford back in for the Royal horses.

"Game Spirit was one of the better rides I'd taken over from Terry and also Aly Branford but for a while it looked as if I might loose the mount. He took some knowing and as Aly had looked good on him when running Pendil to half a length at Newbury while my injures mended. Fulke thought I did not hit it off with the big chestnut when he again met his match at the hands of a Fred Winter chaser, Soothsayer, at Cheltenham.

We did some intensive schooling at home and I'd taken the pre-caution to ask David Mould if he knew the key. He advised pandering to the old horse (an affectionate phrase, not alluding to age) not to force him to be braver at the jumps. Game Spirit was not unlike a spoilt child in some respects and when talking to and patting him during schooling sessions and even during a race, it made him feel full of confidence. When I kept hold of his head he became brave and would jump the moon but if going for a big jump, he lost confidence in his ability to make it.

Game Spirit was as good a chaser as you will find in any generation. Over two and a half miles around Newbury he reigned supreme he much preferred a level track. For me he stripped at least ten pounds better there than anywhere else.

He'd been beaten by Fred Winter's, Crisp, Pendil and Soothsayer at different times then we got one back in Newbury's Hermitage Chase, beating the dual Champion Hurdler Bula in a thrilling contest. Fulke and Fred had only a seven foot brick wall between their stables and you can imagine the rivalry boiled for years.

We discussed tactics with Queen Elizabeth venturing the suggestion that Bula should not be allowed to dominate matters. 'It would be nice to see Game Spirit match strides with Bula all the way' she offered and both Fulke and I were in agreement.

The plan worked as we went at the final four fences in unison at full stretch with no room for error nor any place for the feint hearted. There is no amount of money that could buy the ride on a top chaser going flat out at the last four fences at Newbury, these moments remain burned into the memory for ever.

The last fence loomed up with the usual gathering of racegoing purists standing down there to savour the real taste of chasing. They saw us locked together but Game Spirit flew it the better and fought for every yard of the famous run in with it's dog leg bypassing the water jump. We held on for a narrow but decisive victory to gain the Queen Mother's favourite chaser's ninth win at that course and his twenty first in all.

Newbury saw the end of this magnificent horse on March 5th 1977. Disappointments are a regular shadow in this game but death of an old favourite drains a little more heart out of a rider when it happens.

In this race we could not be worse than second if he ran below par as he always lifted his game here. Asked to carry 12:4 lbs in a field of eight I felt Game Spirit would not fire, there seemed nothing actually wrong with him, he was dull more than anything else.

On pulling up having finished fifth the old horse staggered for only two strides then buckled to the ground and was dead before I'd got to his head.

We had just come off the course onto the walkway back to the unsaddling enclosure, what a blessing he never made it back to the area among the crowds where The Queen Mother was waiting.

The worst side of the sport, Game Spirit died at Newbury after finishing 4th. Everyone is distraught. *(Bernard Parkin)*

Geoffrey Brain the course vet was on hand to see another horse and later his post mortem disclosed cause of death due to a massive haemorrhage of the lungs with signs of previous minor occasions which would have explained his occasional disappointing race.

The Queen Mother told me in her box afterwards that day that she had intended for him to become The Queen's hack, a job he would have done superbly.

We were all very sad yet the lad who looks after a fatality on the course is hit hardest of all. Owner, trainer and jockey each climb into a car and drive off wrapped in their thoughts. The person who looked after the deceased horse had spent twenty times more attention on the horse than even the trainer and at the end of a fateful day they have to pack up it's unwanted tack and sit next to the empty stall in the horsebox going home. Imagine going back to the yard with a bridle, headcollar and rug that just a few hours before had been worn by the horse that they saw more of than their own spouse?

It's so personal, Queen Elizabeth sent for both myself and Peter Payne who looked after Game Spirit. She put her own grief behind her and showed such concern for our feelings, our sense of loss. She is a credit to the human race."

Isle of Man ranks among the best of the Royal owned horses Bill partnered during his years as Walwyn's stable jockey at Saxon House. The well bred, handsome gelding did all his winning at courses close to and including Windsor and Ascot. In Smith's words, "He proved to be a brilliant horse, I thought he would make up into a Cheltenham Gold Cup horse then it became patently obvious he did not stay the trip. We put him back to shorter distances and he was good. In fact he was the best jumper of a chase fence at speed that I've ever sat on, a thrill a minute."

Tammuz, who was bred to be a good flat racehorse is warmed up just before the off, when winning The Shweppes Gold Trophy in 1975. *(Bernard Parkin)*

They come with all sorts of attributes or quirks and as good a jumper as Isle of Man was, Tammuz showed the opposite ability to get from one side of a jump to the other.

"He had awful legs, Fulke performed miracles to keep him going, that may have contributed to his not liking to get airborne. When he met one on a good stride, he'd jump well but once he was in top gear or out on his own, he'd flatten obstacles. During his time with us two different operations had to be done on his legs to keep him sound.

In 1974/75 season he came back after a year's forced absence, had an educational jaunt at Sandown, won at Kempton Park on Boxing Day and because he could quickly become stuffy winded, appeared again at Wincanton in January to keep him right for the Schweppes at Newbury the next month. We ran four in the race and if there is any such thing as a certainty, Tammuz was it. Leaving nothing to chance I walked the course the evening before the big race to find the best of the going up the final straight came under the stands rails. That would be my path.

Going to the front with two hurdles to jump, Tammuz stepped on the last jump and flattened it but held the late challenge of Legal Tender by half a length. As he idled a bit when in front, I had to give him a couple of slaps to keep the valuable prize even though the Queen Mother's jockeys were under strict instructions to only use the riding aid when absolutely necessary. It was.

We tried to make a chaser of him but Tammuz had other ideas.

Around this time Fulke and I had a serious fall out. I fell off one at Kempton, pulled Tammuz up at the same meeting over fences and made it a treble to forget by falling off a second horse, chipping my elbow on one arm and pulling muscles in the other. I was armless when the boss piled into me and it had got so heated that we'd both told the other to get knotted.

I was so mad that I still rode Fort Devon in the next race and despite being a total passenger, won easily. There must be a moral to the story but as it reflects badly on the worth of a jockey, perhaps it is best left unsaid.

Unable to ride for a few days, Fulke took full advantage of my absence to school Tammuz over the big fences which saw him refuse and convinced then it was the horses way of saying he'd had enough, the trainer suggested to the owner that Tammuz be retired.

I came back for rides at the end of the week and amazingly won on Desert Wind and Queen's College at Newbury. It was the nearest Fulke ever came to an apology, although even then he could not quite make it in proper words. I got the drift though and thought a lot of him as I realised how hard it had been to even consider it."

Bill Smith at his best on Special Cargo at Lingfield Park. His fellow riders presented him with this photo as it was how he wished to be remembered.

Bill Smith only twice had the pleasure or perhaps ordeal of schooling horses in front of the Queen Mother at Walwyn's home ground and one almost turned into disaster.

"I'd tried a horse that we wanted to buy from David Tatlow at Stow-On-The-Wold on the way back from racing. The light had gone and snow lay on the ground yet the willing beast even jumped five feet high parallel poles with no ground line to help him judge take off.

Most impressed we took him to Fulke's for a month's trial and days before the decision time elapsed, Queen Elizabeth came down to see the horses and it seemed a good idea to let her watch Winter Flight jump the row of fences.

As I cantered to the first it occurred to me that I could put on a real show for her by jumping as close to the wing of the fence as I dared especially the second as they were standing there only yards away from it. I thought it would be something to remember if on cantering back to the jubilant party, I popped him over the post and rails partitioning off the schooling ground from the gallops to complete the display.

Plans changed rapidly when approaching the second fence, Winter Wind cocked his jaw and all but ran out exactly where the prospective purchaser stood wide eyed recognising the impending situation. A sharp slap down the horse's shoulder and a firm 'jaw breaker' averted disaster and changed my mind about jumping the railings afterwards.

As it turned out the horse could not gallop fast enough to catch cold and disappeared to pastures new."

Throughout this compilation of events spanning The Queen Mother's racing exploits, it continuously surfaces how considerate she is for other people's feelings, always eager to put them at ease and enjoying the natural banter of racing's characters. Smith remembers several situations to illustrate the point.

"The other time we schooled for her went by as planned until we repaired to the Walwyn's lounge for a drink and a chat about future races. The Queen Mother accidentally knocked her Martini onto the carpet sending all present rushing in diverse directions in search of a cloth to mop it up. When we all reappeared from various doors brandishing cloths there she was on hands and knees dabbing at the wet patch with her handkerchief. She looked up and said 'Oh dear, but I do really think it will not stain the carpet now.'

Another occasion I wanted to eat my words, was on dismounting from Isle of Man who side stepped, treading on my toe. Half a ton of horse on paper thin boots is not to be recommended, I screamed at his lad to get the F..ing horse off me and then still F..ing turned around to be inches from The Queen Mother's face to which she just smiled and said 'I do hope he's not hurt you too much'."

Bill's memory is razor sharp as we mention successive horses. "Colman, not a star, an all righter. Master Andrew, totally kinky but lots of ability, Russ Hill, a huge narrow thing like two boards nailed together, moderate. Sun Rising, a very, very, nice horse who needed time like all his sire's stock, Present Arms, bred by the Queen to win a Derby, if he'd had good tyres he'd been tops. Queen's College, half brother to Isle Of Man, his sire was a polo pony. Upton Grey, a big grey yoke. Prince Charles rode him once at Newton Abbot. A large useless boat, I won on him at Newbury and almost fell off him in surprise. Sunyboy, now there's a story....

This one was a terribly hard ride, always seemed to be struggling yet if the jockey could keep riding him he'd finish like a train. Bags of stamina, you could not have got to the bottom of him if you changed jockeys every half mile. Joe Mercer rode him to be placed in the Irish St. Leger for Lady Beaverbrook who was never totally happy when he ran over jumps.

He ended up being a top staying hurdler then retired to Christopher Sweeting's stud at Churchill in Oxfordshire where he became a much sought after stallion.

He'll be best remembered as the Queen Mothers 300th winner when taking the Fernbank Hurdle on television at Ascot, but was also Fulke's 1600th. That figure made us all stop and think, who would have thought another hundred would be added and now she's started the fifth century!"

Special Cargo pops up in different guises during this book and although Bill Smith enjoyed some memorable wins on him, his greatest triumph when snatching the Whitbread Gold Cup in the last gasping strides will remain vivid as the Royal jockey had actually rejected the mount in favour of Walwyn's more fancied Diamond Edge.

"I only ever got off two of Queen Elizabeth's horses to ride a better fancied stablemate and would you believe it, each time my rejected mount beat me!! I chose Menehall over the lunatic Colonius at

Worcester; not only was mine safer he had far superior form. It looked no contest yet that is the beauty of steeplechasing, things are not totally predictable and at the finish only inches separated us with Colonius's impetuous head the one in front.

Likewise, when the Whitbread came around there could not have been any other choice. Diamond Edge had won the same race twice before and had come back to finish second at the Cheltenham Festival after two years sidelined through injury. The ground rode firm and that suited him and went against Special Cargo, there could be only one choice.

I'd been muttering about retiring for a while and had told Fulke that unless something silly such as falling early on or finishing out with the washing, I'd go out smiling that day.

Diamond Edge ran up with the leaders all the way while poor old Special Cargo struggled to keep tabs on us. If you'd backed him you'd have torn up your tickets and gone to the bar for a drink after three miles. Then as he'd done so often before he devoured the hill to the finish and going to the last had got up to fourth place but had used tremendous energy to get anywhere near us.

My battle against Fred Winter's Plundering and Michael Dickinson's Lettoch developed into one of those finishes that go down in racegoers mental notes as the stuff true chases are about. Slowly, desperately Diamond Edge dug into his deepest recourses to get his nose in front yards before the finish to give me the best possible send off to retirement. Yes, we won that battle all right but hidden from my view on the far side of Lettoch the patched up old Special Cargo had flown from nowhere to poke his Roman nose in front on the line to deny me of my greatest hour.

Tired and distraught for a few seconds, I quickly realised the significance of the result. The Queen Mother had gained her biggest success with her favourite horse at her most loved course, what better ending could there be!!

We all congregated in the Royal Box afterwards and The Queen Mother kept on pointing to me on the film saying 'There you are, do look and see how unlucky you were not to win,' you would not have known she had a runner in the race herself let alone won it, she is such an amazing person, she feels for other people with genuine emotion.

She gave a dinner three weeks later for just eight people which included The Queen and Princess Margaret but once more the attention focused on me and Diamond Edge. You don't come across people like that very often more's the pity."

Bill persuades Upton Grey to win at Newbury in 1978 *(Bernard Parkin)*

Bill Smith retired that day after ten years of wearing the Royal colours to 51 victories and a whole host of losers, some unlucky. He walked away somewhat less than sound in limb though fine in brain and heart. He had most of his own teeth, a full head of black hair and a host of memories.

For his wife Sue who had spent many long evenings after putting there two children to bed, waiting for the phone to shrill out the news of another bone crunching fall, retirement came as a blessed relief. They had shared highs and lows and would not have changed it for an oil well.

Bill Smith is now an equine adviser to the Dubai ruling family. It seems Sheikh Mohammed and his entourage do listen to him!

Chapter 12

Aly Branford: The super sub.

Aly Branford stopped the 25 year old tractor and rotavator that have helped him make a living ever since injury forced him out of the jumping game and took me back down memory lane. He spent his time at Fulke Walwyn's stable as second jockey to Terry Biddlecombe and then Bill Smith. Aly got the ride whenever the top man thought more of his skin than the riding fee but whenever they did break or bend enough to keep them out of the saddle, always proved more than up to the task.

In all he rode nine winners for the stable's Royal owner and even through the stubble and stained face after a hard day's landscaping, those glorious moments when the plan went right, shone through.

"You can imagine the excitement when the Queen Mother's horses arrived. We all cast our eyes over them like kids in a chocolate factory.

I rode most of them in their first schooling sessions as I worked in the yard every day. Game Spirit and Isle of Man were the first two and I can remember thinking if that was the quality of the remaining ten, we'd have a sensational season.

When it came to showing them off in public for the first time Terry had not recovered from injury and so David Mould got the call to ride Game Spirit in the Mackeson Gold Cup. You could judge the class of the race as our chap started at 16/1 having won eleven races. As it turned out he ran far better than the bookies thought possible to only fail by half a length to peg back the twice champion two miler Skymas.

Fulke was very loyal to his riders and several times refused to take horses from powerful owners who wanted their own jockeys to ride them. 'If I train the horses, I choose the jockeys!' was his condition and that turned out to be the only time David rode one of ours.

Lt. Col. Sir Martin Gilliat, Private Secretary to the Queen Mother for 4 decades. *(Gerry Cranham)*

Next time he ran, at Newbury the day before Red Candle beat Red Rum in the Hennessy, I got my chance and understandably, I was quite nervous. One or two had past their sell-by dates, others had problems, Game Spirit was definitely her best horse then.

The Guv'nor called me into the office to explain the certain etiquette required when meeting members of the Royal family. 'Remember to bow on approaching, don't put your hand out to shake hands unless she does so first and do not wear gloves.' All these things were going through my mind let alone the race and as I got nearer the spot where Fulke always stood at Newbury. I started my bow but as I was still six or seven paces from The Queen Mother I was almost falling over by the time I got near her.

Of course, I need never have worried because she put me at ease straight away saying 'Well, whatever happens I do hope you have a jolly good ride'. She put absolutely no pressure on me to win, the guv'nor did all that before we got to the races.

I never had a moment's worry in the race, coming home in a canter from Helmsman and Andy Turnell with plenty of time to ease down cheekily."

All was not rosy, however, for the chaser's third run for Walwyn as he decided Terry Biddlecombe would ride the horse. Aly got the call to attend the office where the news rocked him more than a bit. "I asked him how he could jock me off after all the schooling I'd done and then won on our only outing on the racecourse," Aly told me. "Fulke said The Queen Mother had asked for Terry, which of course she hadn't but at the end of the day he was the boss and I went off elsewhere to ride Barmer. He won right enough then dropped dead after passing the post, it's the only time I've come back to the winner's enclosure with a saddle and no horse. The bad feeling between the Guv'nor and myself soon blew over as we were on to other horses and problems. I must admit, though I blew my top at least eight times during the years at Saxon House, we understood each other though and it seemed to work."

Biddlecombe kept the ride and again just failed to give almost two stones away to the good mare Credo's Daughter owned by actors

James Bolam and Susan Jameson. They kept the mare and have been enjoying some decent wins with her son King Credo in the early 90's.

Then he reaped the reward a retained stable jockey sees as his bonus when steering Game Spirit to an armchair victory in a two horse race at Wincanton (at odds of 1/8!!) and another odds on victory at Windsor two weeks later.

The only other race that first season under Walwyn's care saw the big, genuine chaser split the stables trio of runners in the 1974 Cheltenham Gold Cup. Captain Christy and Bobby Beasley returned from two years retirement to win an amazing race from Walwyn's The Dikler with Game Spirit third and Charlie Potheen fourth.

Over that trip Game Spirit was stretched just too far but he reverted to lesser distances to win six more chases and finish second in the Two Mile Champion Chase to Skymas.

By this time Bill Smith had replaced Terry Biddlecome, with Aly Branford still in the supporting role. He only got back on Game Spirit once more in a two horse race against the American horse Soothsayer at Wincanton when the bookies could not split them at 6/4 each of two.

"It was not a happy return either. The old horse became a bit windy when the ground was slippery and would balloon his fences losing no end of ground in the process. John Francome knew our weakness and went off like a dingbat beating us by half a mile. You can imagine Fulke's face, apart from telling me to see him in the office later, he wouldn't even speak to me", Aly laughingly recalled. "There was no such struggle over who should ride Greystoke Pillar though, he was a lunatic, couldn't bend his back so he knocked hurdles out of the way.

Mouldy won three hurdles on him before we got him and Bill Smith notched up one over the smaller obstacles but for his novice chasing stint guess who became the flavour of the month?

We did win twice but it's the ones we failed to finish that stick in the memory. In a two horse race at Ludlow Sandy May on one of David Barons' novices agreed not to take me on over the first few fences. A sort of airy fairy leap at the first did not fill me with a lot of confidence which mattered little as we fell at the next, would you credit it bringing Sandy down on top of us! Fifty feet wide the second fence is and he could still not miss me.

Both horses got up before us only to gallop off into the distance past the stands where David Barons jumped over the rails and caught Sandy's horse and brought it back for him to remount. I prayed no one would catch mine.

I stayed down lying in the grass hoping if they did catch it they'd decide I was not fit to remount. Sandy did a lone circuit to come home alone and as he passed me I shouted 'well done' and meant it.

If Colonius met a fence correctly he was brilliant. Aly Branford saw a good stride at Worcester races. May 1975. *(Bernard Parkin)*

Colonius had a lot of similar negative qualities yet we all got our share of glory on him. I got the leg up when Bill Smith was injured, ending up with four wins in the Queen Mother's colours on him.

He used to frighten his riders to death in the early stages as he was always out of control. If you had the nerve to let him run flat out over the first three fences he'd burn off his excess energy and settle a bit. It really did take ten years off my life over the first few fences, the speed and the length of his jump had to be seen to be believed. He fell about the same number of times he won which is rather like you going out in a car that you knew would crash quite often. Despite that, to ride winners for Queen Elizabeth is worth frightening yourself for."

That view is shared by everyone who ever comes in contact with Queen Elizabeth and included two policemen who stopped to enquire why a horsebox was parked on the hard shoulder of the M4 motorway.

Colonius had to travel in a box on his own as he got so excited. This time he'd gone mad and Pete Stanley who looked after him was trying to settle the horse down before he did himself damage. When the two police officers established the identity of the horse's owner they promptly escorted the horsebox right to the course.

Aly Branford accepts the role of second jockey is frustrating. Called to duty when the top man is hurt or riding elsewhere, dropped the moment he returns to fitness or the stable has runners at a solitary meeting.

Of course he could at any time leave for pastures new but better a slice of fresh bread than a whole stale loaf.

Even so it rankles a little to be used as a yo-yo.

The second top class inmate to join Walwyn's yard from Peter Cazalet came in the shape of Isle of Man, a half brother to the reckless Colonius and the very decent Inch Arran who were full brothers. By the Queen Mother's former racehorse Manicou, he came late to the scene and coincidentally won fourteen races, exactly the number won by both his half brothers. If the current breeding mares at Sandringham can match that strike rate we could well see another party for the 450th winner.

Aly got first crack at seeing how good Isle of Man was in November 1973 when as a six year old he made a belated debut only to be headed close home by Fred Winter's Fervor. The rivalry between the two stables separated by a red brick wall had grown to interesting proportions, to beat the other then counted for double a normal victory.

Biddlecombe replaced Aly for the gelding's second run at Cheltenham the following month where once again the horse found one too good. This time it happened to be Col. Bill Whitbread's Our Edition, trained by Stan Mellor and although Fulke did not like second place, no one was happier than Queen Elizabeth whose friendship with the Colonel is legendary.

Aly did get back on the horse he'd started off when tried over fences with the pair winning well at Sandown Park but then he had to take a watching brief as Bill Smith made the horse his ride, winning a further ten chases.

That particular Sandown win on Isle of Man came among a treble for him with The Queen Mother's Present Arms also obliging to make him a headliner for a change.

Present Arms had been a present from The Queen and but for untrainable front legs could have gone right to the top. "It's all so terribly easy when you have the right material." he pointed out. "I rode no better or worse that day yet the press thought I'd been brilliant. Fulke was pleased and the owner ecstatic."

Colonello also inherited from the Cazalet stable, never made it to the course from Walwyn's yard after doing his best to turn inside out at regular intervals. "He had a screw loose", Aly shivered. "Unpredictable, described him. Going onto the sand gallop the second day we cantered him he appeared sweet enough then without warning or provocation he did a U-turn and I found myself being carted down the lane to the yard.

When we tried to school him in the paddock behind the stables he just ran off and buried both of us in the ten foot high thorn hedge that marks the boundary.

Give the Guv'nor his due, he mumbled that the horse was a lunatic and he'd not risk my neck any more. Jack O'Donoghue then had the dubious pleasure of working his animal magic on Colonello which he did when winning a novice chase at Sandown under his Welsh jockey Charlie Goldsworthy.

That double turned out to be my last Royal winners as the next season I broke an arm and a wrist at Ascot. In those days there used to be a good chase there on a flat race day. I'd been up at Aintree for The Topham Trophy on the Thursday to partner Pakie for the stable owned by Andrew Parker Bowles. He only ever lasted two or three races a year due to unsoundness. I tried to get off him to ride for Richard Head, he had a favourite's chance but Fulke rightly made me stick to ours. Josh Gifford's brother Macer took the ride.

Macer fell at the first fence and then two more went at the third jump, the Chair. I missed the fallers and jumped around to finish an honourable second.

With Macer out I asked to ride his Ascot mount which also turned a double somersault crushing my arm and wrist. He'd ridden my horse and I'd ridden his and, ironically, neither of us ever rode again.

In the race that ended my career, twelve started, three finished. Ron Atkins who'd fallen early, had the fright of his life when running onto the course to cheer us on during the second circuit. He was mown down a second time by his own horse and this time he did the job properly being carted off to hospital with the rest of us.

As second jockey, Aly Branford had to take the rough with the smooth.
(Bernard Parkin)

With so many injured jockeys there for treatment at once my arm was set rather quickly and crudely and after three months it became obvious the healing had not taken place. It all dragged on for a year which eventually forced me to accept at the age of 30 there were only a couple of good years in me anyway.

With not enough money to set up training it slowly dawned upon me to do something different, landscaping came out best. As I only owned a fork and spade it seemed I would be busy enough without making enough to live on, so the Injured Jockeys Fund under Edward Courage provided me with the second hand tractor and rotovator and I banged on local's doors.

Fred Winter gave me my first jobs and it grew from there. Landscaping may sound quite grand but there's more muck than money.

I did enjoy my racing, it took me to places I'd never have been otherwise and of course allowed me to ride for The Queen Mother.

She is so good at putting people at their ease I even plucked up more courage than when riding her Colonello, to suggest a contract to do the window boxes at Clarence House. She seemed quite amused at the proposition but I'm still waiting for the call."

"I'm perfectly able to hold my hat on gentlemen." *(Gerry Cranham)*

Chapter 13

Kevin Mooney:
Local lad makes good

Kevin Mooney was born in Lambourn, served his apprenticeship with Barry Hills on the flat in the village, got enough excitement and glory riding Queen Elizabeth's horses trained there by Fulke and retired from the saddle to rejoin Barry Hills as assistant trainer. He is truly a man of the Valley of the Horse.

Kevin saw his chance when stable jockey Bill Smith and the chaser Tarbank failed to gel. Bill had the mother and father of a fall at the first fence on the schooling ground and when ordered by Fulke Walwyn to try again, flatly refused to do so. He did, however, agree to ride his least favourite horse in a race at Kempton Park in the hope it would find some reason to live when geed on by the public occasion. Such positive thinking sadly was rewarded by another burial when Tarbank turned upside down at the very first fence. Having convinced himself and Walwyn there looked to be no future in that particular partnership, Kevin Mooney came in for the dubious pleasure of trying his hand and decided he'd prefer to go straight to the course without frightening either of them schooling at home.

"Bill Smith had a ride in the race at Newbury when I had my first ride on Tarbank. After a bit of banter from him Bill did say if we survived the first fence he thought we'd win, on the face of his two previous attempts over fences that looked distinctly unlikely! Tarbank did survive to finish a gallant second beaten just half a length and in doing so elevated me in the guv'nor's eyes. The down side of such a break is that every half crazy, poor sighted, bad legged moderate jumper all of a sudden becomes your ride," Mooney laughed.

"The first time I wore The Queen Mother's colours was on a moderate little horse called Colman at Hereford in a contest restricted to jumping apprentices. We finished second which was as good as the horse would ever be but to me the moment will remain vivid for ever. To walk out to the parade ring in those silks elevates a rider beyond belief.

The Queen Mother with Kevin Mooney at Ascot 1988.
"The perfect stable jockey" said Michael Oswald.   *(Bernard Parkin)*

My first winner in the Royal silks came on a former Dick Hern flat horse called Cranbourne Tower at Windsor with the owner present. The guv'nor just introduced me to her in the tree lined parade ring and left me to it. I'd never even met The Queen Mother when she'd been down to the yard so you can imagine I was rooted to the spot but she

Michael Oswald K.V.O. loves fast jets as much as he does managing the Royal Studs and the Queen Mother's jumpers.

The Queen Mother has always been a colourful character and enjoys those she meets.

Charles Radclyffe tells the Queen about the youngsters. The Queen Mother is open coated despite the wintry day.

Good staff are hard to find. New Zealand's leading race caller Keith Haub often calls in to lend a hand at Kim Clotworthy's stables.

Breeding for the future the Queen Mother's mares and foals have space to grow at Sandringham. (Mandy Pitman).

At Sandringham Last Romance and her 1994 colt foal. "The pick of the bunch." (Mandy Pitman).

The Queen Mother loves to see her horses on the gallops as well as at the races, Nicky Henderson holds Nearco Bay in October 1994. (Bernard Parkin).

Five of the Queen Mother's horses being prepared by Mary Crouch prior to joining the Royal trainers. Nearco Bay in centre.

Charles Radclyffe drives one of the Queen Mother's yearlings as part of their breaking in process. (Mandy Pitman).

Vet, Bobby McEwan on The Argonaut leads his wife Ali out hunting on former New Zealand Olympic 3 day eventer Tempo.

The Ascot Luncheon to celebrate the Queen Mother's 400th winner.

"Well Mother - what do you think? Shall we ask them to trot up and down once more? I'm sure they've being over indulging. (Bernard Parkin).
(Left to Right. Michael Oswald, Sir Piers Bengough and the Earl of Carnarvon).

chatted away as if she'd known me all my life, she is the most natural and charming person.

Cranbourne Tower had looked useful on the flat being placed at Royal Ascot and had jumped well at home. He duly won, filling me with immense pride and although it was the Queen Mother's 323 rd winner, you would have thought it was her first. She really does love the game and never ever treated me any differently after disappointments either.

Cranbourne Tower did manage to win another hurdle the next season, again at Windsor, before I lost the ride to Bill Smith, who added a novices' chase at Worcester to his score.

It took three years before I got another chance to add to my Royal tally of two. This came about again because of my role of Kamikaze pilot when Lundale arrived from Sandringham.

This great big woolly thing came out of the horsebox with his eyes on stalks and as it was obvious he'd be my ride, I was given the horse to look after in the stable. He was as nutty as he looked, the first time I ventured to put a saddle on him he reared over backwards, fell out of the stable and ran riot around the yard with the Guv'nor waving his arms like a demented windmill to try to stop him.

He turned out to be a crank, we had to put a special bridle on him to get some power assisted steering although that only worked half the time.

Chris, who rode him out most days, used to disappear at some stage every day. Without warning Lunedale would stick his head up and away from the rider which gave control to the horse. He knew just the right angle to put his head so that the rider became the passenger and would charge off into the wide blue yonder no matter what was in the way.

As we could not be sure what Lunedale would do on the racecourse, it was decided to run him at Stratford On Avon purely because The Queen mother could not go that particular day.

The Guv'nor was in a real twitchy mood and even pulled my golf ball air freshener off the mirror and threw it out of the window as it annoyed him. If he felt nervous, how on earth did he think I felt!

As it happened, Lunedale behaved quite well to finish fourth, good enough to persevere with. He managed to win a couple of novice hurdles at Stratford the next term but you could never trust him, lots of ability but unpredictable and explosive into the bargain. No one else ever rode him on a racecourse, there were no volunteers.

When we put him to fences in 1984 he actually ran out going down the back straight at Sandown Park then once he'd beaten me, did a U-turn which brought him back onto the course a few strides from the fence we'd run out at. He jumped it in a fashion then proceeded to stroll away with the race.

We won the race at Windsor named after our yard which pleased everyone then were aimed specifically at the Royal Game Chase at Sandown as the owner could go that day.

She had not seen him race before but knew his kinks well enough and said to me in the parade ring 'Do please look after yourself, you must be very brave to ride him.' He'd be charging around us when we tried to mount him and then do exactly the same after the race when you would have expected him to be tired. We were worried he'd walk all over the Queen Mother, luckily he never did.

Kevin Mooney gets that elusive first Royal winner for Cath Walwyn, when Royal Pavilion scores at Sandown Park in November 1990. *(Gerry Cranham)*

The first son of Sunyboy, The Queen Mother's 300th winner, to win for her was Sun Rising. He had lots of ability but sadly not a decent leg to carry him. I'd done all the schooling on him and did think I'd get the ride when he ran. However, Bill thought he'd better look after his job and said he'd take over even though he'd never sat on the horse at home. That's life when you're a working jockey, the retained stable rider has the choice.

Bill won a hurdle and a chase in successive seasons with a bout of leg trouble in between and a three year gap for the same after his second win.

Two months later events happened to change my life when Bill chose to ride Diamond Edge instead of The Queen Mother's Special Cargo in the 1984 Whitbread Gold Cup. He'd made up his mind to go out in a blaze of glory and no one could have advised Bill to choose other than Diamond Edge. We'd galloped the two together every work day for a month and you could not get the gap between them to alter, Special Cargo never even smelt which way Diamond Edge had gone.

We took them to Newbury to gallop after racing, then went off to Bath, there was almost a furlong between them. Next stop was Barry Hills' Faringdon Road gallop and this time the old horse did get within twenty lengths of Bill's horse. Again Newbury saw us working after racing but this time it was a set up with Bill strangling his to give mine some confidence and to stop the press from gossiping about the futility of running Special Cargo.

The ground for the Whitbread rode fast and perhaps if it had rained Bill would have changed partners.

Special's old legs looked like corkscrews and always threatened to break down again. How the Guv'nor kept him sound for so long I'll never understand. With this in mind I had orders to pull the old boy up if he felt the ground too firm. On all known form and because of his unsoundness, the horse could not win. He did, which just goes to prove that if you do not run you can't win.

During the race Bill and I exchanged views on our chances and by the time we completed one circuit he said Diamond was making funny noises and I told him old Special was not at all happy on the fast ground. We swung away from the stands and I was left as if standing still, only his jumping kept Special in touch with the rest. Once you turn

Kevin Mooney rode for the Queen Mother an hour after being 'buried' by Ten Plus at Cheltenham. "Shaken and stirred, but not enough to let anyone else ride in the Blue and Buff". January 1988.   *(John Beasley)*

down the back straight there with seven fences in a row jumping counts for a lot. We were flat out with no room for adjustment if we met a fence wrong and going so fast if we'd missed our take off, we'd still be rolling now.

Ping, ping, ping we went all down the back and were on their tails turning into The Pond fence three from home where four horses passed me as if flying.

The one thing the Guv'nor had impressed on me before the race was to stick to the inside rail like chewing gum and, sure enough, as the others all fanned out to challenge each other a gap opened up like Moses at the Red Sea. This acted on Special like a turbo charger, he changed legs and quickened which made me think I could run on to be third which was a good result. I was thrilled to bits thinking we'd be placed.

Remembering how he'd eaten up opponents from the last fence here on four previous visits, I gave Special a couple of backhanders with my whip and he sprouted wings. Diamond Edge led, was headed, led again in a desperate battle with Plundering and Lettoch from the last fence with my chap joining the issue on the line. Most people in the stands thought Bill had won but I knew we'd got up and the video shows me punching the air, there was no doubt although the photo finish print showed it to be a desperate affair.

As we joyously lumbered back up the walkway to the winners enclosure Mrs Walwyn reached me first. She had gone for a fair old gamble on Diamond Edge and had convinced herself she'd landed it with me second. When I told her there was no doubt I'd won, she shouted 'You can't have, no you haven't. ...... Have you?'

The reception brought tears to peoples' eyes, the Sandown crowd know what the place and more specifically this race meant to Queen Elizabeth and they threw hats sky high. I'd been used to looking at others riding in to the winner's enclosure, to see it from the other angle made me feel ten feet tall.

The Queen Mother was marvellous and in her usual manner she wanted to talk more about the luckless Diamond Edge's narrow defeat than her own victory. She kept saying 'How unfair, they should not be split. It should be a dead heat. Poor Diamond Edge, poor Bill.'

In the end her concern was quelled as the judge ruled the print gave second place to Lettoch, only two nostrils separated the three horses after a race that could not be bettered for changing fortunes and a show of raw courage. How apt that The Queen Mother should come out on top in such an epic battle as she has displayed exactly that throughout her long involvement in the sport.

One thing that winning for the Royal family does is to take someone like me to places money cannot buy. Leading businessmen may attract honours but few will ever earn an invitation to small Royal parties such as the one given after the Whitbread. There were only eight people dining, The Queen, The Queen Mother, Princess Margaret, Colonel Whitbread, Fulke and Mrs Walwyn, Bill Smith and myself.

After coffee the men swapped tales while the ladies retired to other rooms for ten minutes before rejoining us to view old videos of memorable races. To this day I can hardly believe how relaxed everything was as The Queen herself just sat down on the carpet to watch the television not six inches from my shoes.

Bill retired as he had intended and the first job became mine. I will always be grateful to Her Majesty for allowing me to assume the mantle as she could have asked for any jockey, gone for a more fashionable rider.

It was such an important step to me, Sun Rising was pencilled in as the first opportunity and as luck would have it I got well and truly buried the day before in a modest chase at Taunton. There I was, having attained the honour of being the Royal jump jockey, battered and bruised all over to such an extent that it looked increasingly as if I would not be fit to carry out my duty at Newbury the next day.

I had physiotherapy that night and again in the morning but my spine felt as if the vertebrae were made of glass splinters. It was so important to ride for the Queen Mother that I'd have ridden whatever the discomfort. The trouble with this particular horse though, was he never ever took hold of the bit. He was so idle I had to push and kick from start to finish to make him do any work and on this, his steeplechasing debut, I rode him like a sack of spuds.

Sun Rising ran well enough to finish third pleasing The Queen Mother, although the Guv'nor did ask me what the hell I thought I was playing at.

He'd been pretty lazy before but after three years doing nothing except eat his head off, he'd become clever and was taking the Mickey. Basically the horse needed blinkers to make him do his best. Fulke would not put them on saying The Queen Mother would not like to see her horses in blinkers as it usually indicated a coward. My persistent reasoning angled that without them to help sharpen the horse up I'd have to be too hard on him and that would be even worse in her eyes. Eventually, after a couple of wins at Ascot and Wincanton where I ended up being sick from physical exhaustion, Sun Rising got the blinkers to complete a four timer within the space of two months including in The Rip Chase, named after The Queen Mother's former horse.

That day The Queen and Princess Margaret accompanied The Queen Mother, it is something else I shall never forget.

Both Sharron my wife and myself come from ordinary families and to have been The Queen Mother's jockey has given us something so far removed from our dreams that we would not have presumed to have thought it possible."

Sired after his dam visited the Equine Fertility Unit at Newmarket. 'The Ugly Duckling', Dudley with Kevin Mooney.

Michael Oswald summed up Kevin Mooney's contribution, "He was the ideal stable jockey, loyal and true. Kevin always took the shortest route around the inside and was sympathetic to our horses."

Kevin Mooney retired in 1991 specifically to join Barry Hills as assistant trainer. He lives in the village he was born in and is as contented a man as I have seen for many a year and that is due in the main to knowing he would be hard pushed to ever better the time he spent wearing the Blue and Buff which yielded nineteen Royal winners.

Chapter 14

Ian Balding:
Trainer to two Queens

For two decades prior to becoming one of Queen Elizabeth's jumping trainers, Ian Balding had the honour of handling her daughter Queen Elizabeth II's flat race horses, albeit numerically second to Major Dick Hern.

The Queen's home bred Insular became the first hurdler the charming, Peter Pan like, trainer oversaw for her mother. The gelding did not make the racecourse as a two year old, then made a healthy contribution to The Queen's tally at three when winning the last four of his seven starts.

"Seems to act on any going; a progressive sort who should win more races" were Timeform's thoughts on the horse at the end of his first season.

They turned out to be correct as he proceeded to win once again the next term as well as filling the runner up's spot four times. "probably finds one and a half miles the bare minimum these days; good ride for an apprentice" was the less encouraging prediction this time.

As a five year old Insular gained two further wins and several placings including in The Queen's Vase at Royal Ascot, which in Lord Carnarvon, The Queen's racing manager's eyes, made him hurdle race material. Ian Balding leapt at the chance to dabble with jumpers

"He's entitled to be tired", the Queen Mother tells Ian Balding, after Insular won the Wood Speen Hurdle at Newbury in 1985. *(Gerry Cranham)*

as the winter game was his birthright.

The Queen suggested to Michael Oswald, twenty five years Stud and Racing Manager to The Queen Mother, that it made sense to leave the horse with Ian Balding as he already knew the horse inside out. This nudge proved all the encouragement Balding needed and soon his Derby winning patron Paul Mellon's black and yellow colours were also seen around Britain's winter courses with a deal of success tempered by equal misfortune.

"There was never any suggestion the horse would run over hurdles for The Queen, that is very definitely her mother's domain. The Queen so obviously enjoys the pleasure her mother finds from her sport and is at pains to take a back seat whenever the Queen Mother gives a racing party. She tries not to miss them and will suddenly appear unannounced to mingle with her mother's guests. When it is a Queen Mother affair, The Queen is very much a guest herself and does enjoy the changed role because usually it is she who is centre stage. I think The Queen is able to be herself at such functions which is a rarity as Monarch", Ian Balding ventured.

"At one such gathering I was amazed when chatting to The Queen Mother, she said 'Oh, Ian, I see you're still riding in point to points,' and I replied 'Well Ma'am no one is supposed to know about that. My two biggest supporters, The Queen and Paul Mellon think I should not risk my neck simply to satisfy my search for thrills with such good flat horses to look after at home.' I had been telling her all about Ross Poldark who I wanted to ride in The Foxhunters' Chase at Aintree when it became obvious her gaze had gone off my eyes to something behind me. As I had my back to the mantelpiece it made me wonder what had caught her interest then she said quietly, 'Ian, would you like a drink? There is a decanter of port behind you and I think we both might have a glass.' It was the way she said it, relaxed and wanting her guest to share a drink with her like any other hostess in the land."

Ian never did manage to ride for The Queen Mother although the one time the opportunity presented itself he lost out to elder brother Toby, "The Duke of Beaufort asked Father if either of us would ride this rather difficult horse she had running in a point to point. Even though I was getting much more riding than Toby, my father's sense of the correct thing to do prevailed and he thought the honour should go to the eldest son. It pulled like hell for two miles, then when the steam ran out it retreated even faster than it had accelerated going to the first fence out of control.

Insular was a bit of an ugly duckling really although he matured into the most consistent of horses under both codes. His front legs turned out like Charlie Chaplin's and I'm afraid gave us numerous headaches. He's here now turned out in one of the paddocks, retired as nanny to our young horses. You ought to see him lording it over the youngsters, I'll bet he's telling them of how it was done in his day, just like old jockeys do to apprentices over a pint in the pub.

He is still an old funk now aged fifteen. I knew he'd get in a state when asked to be one of the horses parading for The Queen Mother's 400th winner party at Ascot racecourse in October 1994, so I took him on a practice ride in the horsebox the week before. We put him on the automatic horses exerciser, rugged him up to get his coat looking better and the day before was satisfied he looked fit for a Queen.

The Queen and The Queen Mother with Michael Oswald and Ian Balding, admire Insular at the 400 Winner Lunch at Ascot. *(Gerry Cranham)*

When I got to Ascot a nasty shock awaited me. The old devil thought he had been brought out of retirement and had sweated, worried himself into a frenzy and had covered himself in a lather. There was precious little time but I washed him all over and he settled marvellously for the parade and I was so proud of him. Princess Margaret, who quietly fancies the role of photographer, did mention that the horses were too fidgety while she took snaps for the family album but each of them had got the message that they were back on the turf where they'd fought out many famous battles. Even so, I though they all behaved better than could be expected, although I did hold my breath when The Queen Mother insisted on wandering amongst them but that is one of the reasons she has stayed in racing, she is a hands on owner, she really does have an affinity with her horses."

This parade brought back so many memories from his racing days. Insular had no fight at all on his hurdling debut at Balding's local track at Newbury in November 1985 when clear from the fourth hurdle, coming home by an easy five lengths under Brian Reilly who is now a starter's assistant.

Beaten nearly ten lengths next time out behind the top juvenile First Bout was no disgrace and proved good enough to make him favourite for his Kempton Park, Boxing Day outing under a new rider, Peter Scudamore. After his customary front running tactics Insular tamely gave way to trail in a well beaten fifth of the nine finishers.

Ian Balding decided a holiday would not come amiss as the gelding had gone straight from a busy flat season to hurdles. It turned out to be the correct move and while he rested the handicapper dropped Insular's rating considerably, letting him in for the valuable William Hill Imperial Cup with only 10 stones 2 lbs on his back. With yet another new jockey, Eamon Murphy claiming 4 lbs allowance, the old warrior who had carried that sort of weight on the flat, must have thought he'd been let loose without a rider. He won but more of that later.

Insular continued his dual purpose role running on the flat for the Queen and over hurdles for the Queen Mother up until the age of eight but in between he also earned his trainer a handsome prize.

"Henry Carnarvon decided the old horse had probably served his owners as well as he could and offered him to me first before exploring other avenues. You have to remember with the Royal Studs continuing to produce fifteen or so new horses each year, decisions have to be made to cull some.

Despite being absent from the flat for the whole of 1987 the old horse continued to work well as a lead horse to my flat horses and I thought it only right to give him some fun on the racecourse. Timeform put on a valuable and prestigious charity day at York each year and in 1988 decided to honour The Queen Mother by naming an amateurs' race after her. Reg Griffin phoned several times to persuade me to enter Insular which in the end I did. At the time I had not transferred him to my ownership, so said to Henry he could still run for The Queen with Princess Anne riding for her. 'Certainly not!' came the immediate reply, 'He's in your colours now and it is your responsibility'. I've never forgotten that day, Insular was given the perfect ride by The Princess to win handsomely, lifting the £10,000 first prize for me. It was somewhat embarrassing at the time yet all concerned were pleased."

That same year the versatile gelding won a novice chase at Exeter in September on hard ground having been leased back to The Queen Mother. This win provided the eight times champion Peter Scudamore with his solitary victory in The Queen Mother's silks and to this day Scu is adamant he'd have swapped any of his major race successes for this modest contest. "The fact that my father had also ridden a winner for The Queen Mother added to the pleasure this win gave me." Scu pointed out "We are the only father and son to have done such a thing. I'd been down to Kingsclere several times to school Insular over fences and loved every moment of the experience. Ian has without doubt the best private training facilities in the country."

The trainer was delighted to win another race for The Queen Mother, "The pleasure one gets from giving her pleasure is just inexplicable. She simply bubbles over with genuine excitement and that is infectious. To be involved with her victories is such a fulfilling thing."

Insular won so very easily that day, having been left with no real threat after Wild Geese departed at the last fence, yet fate frowned once again on him when the tendon that runs down over the hock slipped off somewhat like a bicycle tyre coming off the wheel rim. His active service was over.

As it happened, Ian had to wait four years before taking charge of another jumper for The Queen Mother when Lunabelle, also, home bred at Sandringham, won her novice hurdle at Wincanton on Boxing Day 1992 under yet another jockey gaining his first Royal win, Jimmy Frost.

The mare returned from the race with heat in one foreleg, was rested and repeated the injury the next season when winning her first novice chase.

When Balding phoned the Queen Mother's racing manager Michael Oswald that evening to relay the mixed news, he replied "I can't believe it. D'you know we've got twelve horses in training and eleven of them have got leg problems." There could be no better horse owner though to accept such a run of setbacks as The Queen Mother had seen far worse over the previous forty years. "How sad for Ian," was her instinctive reply on hearing of the reversal. The time spent repairing jumpers is so much more than on the flat and Michael Oswald reflects that in 1993 the Royal jumping string had over 100% set backs, as all the horses were off at least once and several had two bouts of injury or viral problems.

Only two months before Lunabelle's win Queen Elizabeth had visited the stables to watch the mare work on a foul day when the wind and rain lashed the open Downland regardless of who wanted to be out that day.

Ian remembers being concerned for her "Wearing a light blue dress and open necked cotton coat with three quarter inch heeled shoes. She refused any offers of a raincoat and boots only to jump out of my car and head off across the gallop in the long wet grass. She must have got soaking wet feet but insisted she'd be fine with her walking shoes on."

Conversely, The Queen dresses for the weather with a mack, scarf and boots when watching horses on the Downs in the winter.

Two more flat racehorses were then tried over hurdles, both of which had incurred slight tendon strains on the flat, not an enviable situation to start with. Moat Garden is a seriously good horse who could emulate Insular by winning an Imperial Cup one day, while Bass Rock is also well above average. Yes, there are plenty more winners yet to come in The Queen Mother's colours from Kingsclere Stables, providing the wheels stay airtight.

Having so far only worked with former flat racehorses Ian is looking forward to training Bewitch, an unraced four year old who he will start off in 'bumper' races before working through the grades to steeple-chaser. This striking bay filly is a product of The Queen Mother's current band of mares at Sandringham who represent the future in her quest to win a race at the Cheltenham Festival, if not The Gold Cup itself.

Michael Scudamore winning on Gay Record in The Queen Mother's colours. His son Peter won on the Ian Balding trained, Insular, in the same colours to become the only father and son to do so.

Fit For A Queen

Chapter 15

Away from the Racecourse:
Raynham to Letcombe

The team covers a multitude of quite diverse people and locations in order to feed trainers with the end product, a horse fit and sound enough to stand the rigours of training and racing.

Often people who have never ventured into deepest Norfolk think of the county as flat and boring. Generalisation is a dangerous thing at the best of times and in this instance it is an incorrect assumption.

Raynham, the home of Lord Townshend, set among the most beautiful parkland about sixteen miles south east of Sandringham towards Fakenham, provides the space and facilities for the youngstock to grow on and the older warriors to lick their wounds.

Special Cargo has spent his retirement there apart from a five day stint in Newmarket as the intended hack for Henry Cecil. He lords it over the rest from the foals to walking wounded or is willing to nanny horses needing a protective wing. This all goes on under the watchful eye of Sylvia Palmer who has been manager there since 1972.

Officianados in the Arab horse world would be aware of Raynham as the home of The Sky Arabian Stud, which for years played a leading part in breeding and racing these handsome horses from which the modern day thoroughbred descended.

Special Cargo in retirement at Raynham. Did he serve that mare? He's not admitting to anything.

Too often a winning horse's trainer is accredited with not only being a genius for producing the animal fit on the day but most times as if he or she owned it as well.

This is down to the fact that the press and media meet the trainers daily and often would not know the owner if they were standing next to each other. If this situation is irksome, imagine the hurt pride of the army of people who rear or prepare those winners for trainers to finish off.

In Sylvia Palmer's case she has come a full circle, having started off as groom/work rider at Hodcott stables in West Ilsley, owned by The Queen. Then the incumbent was R.J Colling who prior to Sylvia and her friend Susan Fawcett being employed, had never risked any female staff. Now the fairer sex constitute over half of the workforce.

Since 1984 when Eldred Wilson gave up his involvement as head-master to the Royal recruits, The Queen Mother has used the Raynham facilities and that is where her current batch of young stock are maturing. Sylvia Palmer chuckles still at the incidents which at the time were far from amusing.

"They are all such individuals, ever changing and never uninteresting, although some do tend to stick in the mind more than others. Rudolf, named by Queen Elizabeth as his head and nose were abnormally large, always seemed to be in trouble.

He had the worst parrot mouth I've seen and at one stage as a foal looked as if he would have to be put to sleep. His deformed jaw did not effect his eating capabilities though and he thrived, only to badly injure his stifle as a three year old when again given little chance of recovering.

He responded to treatment and lived to get into further mischief when a knee repeatedly filled up like a football.

He could be relied on to be in the thick of things so when a bunch of two year olds and Lunabelle, then a yearling, took fright on Guy Fawkes night, it came as no surprise to learn it was Rudolf who led them over a full sized set of post and rails silhouetted in the moonlight.

Some of my staff had just gone to check on the horses and witnessed the stampede into the night. A large search party scoured the area to no avail. We walked and stumbled over endless fields and woods without trace of the escapees.

At dawn two of the staff rode in pursuit, following the hoofprints whilst the rest of us searched by car. The horses had travelled over four miles almost in a circle having crossed several roads ending up not far from here grazing quite contentedly, looking smug and without a scratch on them.

Rudolf also instigated a rumour that had the National press scurrying up here, even bribing the staff to show them which horse was Special Cargo. The most persistent reporter finally gave up after days of harassing us in the yard, little realising the horse he so desperately wanted to photograph had been inches away sneezing all over his silk suit all the time he'd been in the yard.

The interest in the then retired chaser emanated from Rudolf's inability to recognise the fact his breeding tackle had been removed. He had been spotted covering another yearling and as a precaution we immediately separated the fillies and the geldings but put old Special Cargo in with the girls for company. The locals heard the covering story, saw Special Cargo among them and very soon the story had become fact with the retired Whitbread hero definitely accredited with the secret of prolonged active life.

Another to keep his nick name when registered for racing was Dudley. This one came as rather a surprise to all of us as his dam had failed to get in foal for several years, so she went to The Equine Fertility Unit at Newmarket. During their research into fertility she was mated with a variety of breeds and whatever they did to improve her fertility, it must have worked as years after she left us, a message came back that the E.F.U. had a yearling by Owen Dudley out of the Queen Mother's mare, what should be done with it?"

Michael Oswald takes up the story. "We went to see Dudley and mark my words he looked like a cardboard cut out of a horse he was so narrow. There was not enough room at Sandringham so Raynham got him. The late Lady Townshend, who knew a lot about horses and was not shy when giving her views, said she did not want such a dreadful looking thing in her park either but she warmed to him as everybody did.

He always did clumsy things like standing on people's toes yet nobody held it against him. When he went down to Charles Radclyffe's to be educated before going into training, he utterred 'Good Lord! What on earth is this?' When Charles is not impressed with a horse he just keeps muttering 'Good Heavens, Good Lord'. Dudley had a huge plain head like an old boot. Charles manfully took him on and taught him to jump. He did win at Folkestone but honestly he was not very talented.

Her Majesty saw a lot of him up here and in fact joined in the fun when we made jokes about him, although she would defend him fiercely if we went too far. Like most people, she fell for his helpless charm.

Dudley's feet were troublesome which meant going down to Newmarket for treatment. The girl who looked after him there adored him so we gave him to her, he's lived like a Lord ever since, horribly spoilt and totally happy.

Moat Garden also led the gang assuming the role of herd boss and protector. When changing paddocks a bunch of a dozen horses being wintered out but of course being stuffed with oats, normally prove no trouble being eager to explore the new surroundings. They appeared to be going through from one field to the other in an orderly fashion when one filly darted back to the place she had thought of as home while the rest cantered off to their feed bowls. Moat Garden looked up from his feed, saw the filly in the other paddock and galloped off to the railings separating them. After whinnying at each other for a few seconds, he led her back along the railings to the open gate then escorted her to the rest of the horses, he took his role as lead stallion seriously."

The Queen Mother goes to see her horses at Raynham whenever she is at Sandringham which is usually in mid summer and sometimes Christmas. The Queen also shows an interest, especially if some of her former flat race horses have gone back there on holiday or convalescence.

When she accompanied The Queen Mother to see how the latest group of jumping bred horses had shaped up, one foal she had not seen before caught her eye and elicited a remark that displays the kind of humour and leg pulling that would be present among close knit parents and children throughout the land.

The horse, Sunshine Flight, had inherited his sire, Sunyboy's proliference of white on his head and legs. The Queen and The Queen Mother mirthfully agreed he looked rather like a Fresian cow .

When he reached racing age, which for Sunyboy's took twice as long as more precocious stallions, Sunshine Flight proceeded to run only as fast as a cow and after several attempts yielding one placing, he was found a home with the Parker family in Kent as a show jumper. This suits the gelding who has to date only knocked down three of the two hundred jumps he has faced in public to date. At this stage the 'Fresian Cow' is just out of novice company but one day he could make it among the names at the Horse of the Year Show.

Of the current band of home breds that have been reared at Raynham, the strong, well related gelding Montrose is lucky to be in the land of the living, let alone heading off for the next stage of his education with Nicky Henderson in Lambourn.

Sylvia Palmer explains, "He was born with a fault in one of his guttural pouches which meant he could not release air properly. The vet inserted a tube into the faulty valve which extended out of the colt's nose.

He arrived here after being weaned from his mother, complete with tube sticking out of one nostril. Occasionally it would work itself out

Sylvia Palmer as a stable girl, leads up Borgia for trainer R. J. Colling.

Bold Romeo, 2 year old, by Bold Owl out of First Romance at Raynham with Sylvia Palmer R.V.M. in 1994.   *(Mandy Pitman)*

causing the guttural pouch to block and his throat to blow up making him look just like a Gerbil. The vet had to reinsert it as it evidently was a difficult procedure.

You cannot be with your horses every hour of the day although you do get tuned into every noise and movement. I had been walking around the stables at eleven o'clock one evening doing my last check of the day when I came across Montrose lying down showing the white of his eyes in obvious distress and hardly breathing as the apparatus had blocked his tubes.

Quickly pulling it out of his throat, I was relieved to watch him recover almost at once. Imagine though, had it happened after I'd completed my rounds, he would have suffocated during the night.

The vet operated on him with a laser, opening up the deficient pouch and he has never looked back.

Probably because he's been here the longest and had proved so brave and good on the racecourse, Special Cargo rates everybody's favourite. The Queen Mother relived his famous last gasp victory in the Whitbread Gold Cup when up here in the summer to give him some carrots. She said 'It was such an exciting race, he nearly gave me a heart attack', showing that her outward calm belies an inward turmoil the same as any other horse lover watching their chasers in full flight.

People do not believe it but horses do recognise a friendly voice. Cargo definitely does with his owner and what's more treats her with a gentleness that he reserves just for the one person. There is no head butting when The Queen Mother gives him his carrots.

He gets the call for big occasions. We spruced him up for his owner's 90th birthday parade on Horseguards parade where, aged 17, he stood for hours without putting a foot wrong despite the milling crowds and continuous guns firing. In complete contrast three years ago at Sandown Park for the Whitbread Silver Jubilee he knew exactly where he was and practically turned himself inside out. He excelled as a racehorse there and I'm sure got the buzz that he'd felt so many times before.

He has always been first up to me when I do the rounds of the paddocks and nudges so hard he would push a grown man over if not prepared for the blow. Even so when we went to fetch him in to smarten him up, the artful dodger would not come near us. When his love of food eventually overrode his willfulness, he'd take the carrot and whip around before we could get the headcollar on him.

After a weeks abortive attempts including doped food and with the event getting too close for comfort, I took all his companions away to other fields and left the gate open. Nosiness got the better of him after a while and he wandered into the stable yard with an air of 'What's going on then, have I missed anything'."

There is a great competition among the Newmarket trainers regarding the best hack to watch daily gallops from. Special Cargo looked a prize specimen in this area and Henry Cecil got in first. There were many tearful eyes at Raynham the morning he departed for the wide open spaces of Newmarket heath and the pampering Cecil's inmates get. Within five days the old horse was back at Raynham and has lorded it among the parkland ever since.

Henry is too long at the game to go jumping on a new horse without concrete evidence that it will not upset his breakfast or rearrange his looks, so for the first few days nannying the string Special Cargo had head lad Paddy Rudkin on board.

Sitting quietly by Warren Hill, Paddy eyed the new intake of two year olds stretching out past him. After the fourth of the twenty in that string had passed, Special Cargo decided that was what racehorses were meant to do and no one had told him he'd retired so he took off with Paddy, joined in with the string and beat them all up to the end of the gallop where an unjumpable hedge confronted them. The thought of his mount's former exploits around Sandown Park caused Paddy to opt for the lesser of the two evils and ejected himself from the saddle in case the old warrior attempted the impossible and took the hedge on.

Henry Cecil never did try to see if his prowess in the saddle matched Special Cargo's mischief! It turned into a case of 'Thanks but no thanks.'

The Queen's personal honour of the Royal Victoria Medal was awarded to Sylvia Palmer in the 1995 New Year's Honours List as recognition of all those freezing wet and windy days when she has put the Royal horses before her own self. Of the dozen recipients of this particular medal, it is noteworthy that only one was granted to a lady, Mrs John Palmer R.V.M.

Pre training work is also carried on further south. Having initially been enlisted by Dick Hern to bring on The Queen's flat horses that were holidaying or coming back from injury, Mary Crouch, whose livery business hums along in Letcombe Regis near Lambourn, also got the call to do the arduous roadwork on the Queen Mother's horses after Peter Cazalet's death.

Nestled under The Ridgeway that runs from Marlborough to the Thames at Pangbourne, this base provides tranquillity and steep hills that are so necessary to get the vital conditioning work into steeple-chasers, fat after months of eating themselves silly on the spring and early summer grass.

A former top Point to Point rider, Mary Crouch has specialised in preparing horses for the army of trainers who use the natural old turf on the adjacent Downland. It is a fluctuating business and when full to bursting, the stable starts the working day long before dawn and in the middle of January there are far more pleasant places to be at 5:30 a.m!

Early risers in the village have got used to seeing the small stirrup lights attached to each horse, bobbing about like fireflies as the string trots briskly through the darkness.

At the same time that the Queen Mother's horses spread to Raynham, Michael Oswald enlisted the services of Charles Radclyffe whose reputation as an equine talent scout, master horseman and jumping teacher, was renowned from the U.K. to America via Ireland and all points south, east and west.

A landowner and farmer in Oxfordshire, Charles runs his horse business in tandem with his farming. Over the past twenty years the leading trainers and owners have both bought horses from him and/or sent their flat horses to be taught to jump in his famous loose school where youngsters can jump 40 obstacles in the space of six minutes. "If Charlie Boy can't make them jump, no one will" has often been heard from those who know.

For twenty odd years, the number of former equine pupils to go from his yard and win the same season have numbered 80 in a normal time and top the century in a good year. Add to that the impressive list of leading chasers and hurdlers that have been selected and bought by him from Ireland as unfurnished yearlings, and you could not fail to be impressed.

"I'm mad for these two" Charles Radclyffe tells Richard Pitman, as they look at some yongsters he bought as yearlings. *(Mandy Pitman)*

Grand National, Gold Cup, Champion Hurdle, Whitbread and any other major race you care to mention, Charles has either bought and sold or made the winner.

Michael Oswald made the perfect choice when he brought Charles and his wife Duse into the team. Not only could he do the required job with the Royal youngsters, he and his wife ran the sort of home and privacy where The Queen Mother could easily relax. She watches her horses jumping loose, is able to evaluate their well being within the confines of a pretty Cotswold stone yard, wander around the paddocks looking at the yearlings and lunch with the type of person she identifies with, engulfed in horsy chat.

"You are left in no doubt when Charles loves or dislikes a horses, the Royal racing manager told me, 'I'm mad for this horse' is the statement we long to hear. 'Oh Heavens, Oh Lord', means the animal is unappealing. He would never dream of running one down through sheer good manners and breeding but his stock phrases tell us all we want to know."

Charles has suffered from his own success and generosity as many of his clients request to measure the exact specifications of his indoor jumping arena in order to erect a replica. Martin Pipe, more used to others copying his innovative ideas has not been too proud to adopt the Radclyffe methods, having benefited from the maestro's services for years, including for his first major success Baron Blakeney in the Triumph Hurdle at the Festival in 1981.

The Radclyffe show stopper when owners go to see what wonders he has worked on their pride and joy, is to bark an order to his head man Patrick Foley who is standing at the horses head, showing the horse in its best light. (Horses and humans all stand to attention at Lew House when working. Manners maketh man and the same applies to horses.)

"Jump on its back, Patrick", Charles decides. "But it's not saddled the disbelieving owner protests". "Doesn't matter, no time for insignificant details like that" he retorts, "Time to go in to the house for a glass of fizz, eh. Patrick, jump the horse over that set of post and rails, there's a good chap."

Without even the slightest hesitation the athletic Foley vaults onto the horses back, turns on its tracks and disappears over the railings then the last you see of the pair is them getting smaller by the minute as they proceed to pop over whatever natural jump is in front of them. No one could fail to be impressed.

I have a sneaking suspicion, the ploy has been well rehearsed and if at all unsure of a successful outcome, the bareback display is dispensed with and it's back to the house for drinks at the double!!

There is no doubt that Charles Radclyffe is a master of the art in persuading horses there is an easy way to jump obstacles, which in turn enables them to gain ground economically. Ground taken from rivals while in the air is far less taxing than the same amount of lengths snatched back by galloping and after a spell at Lew House, horses have been taught exactly how to get out of trouble or better still, not to get into any in the first place.

Even now as a well preserved seventy one year old, the bold Captain takes the reins himself when he feels it necessary to break horses in. The 1994 batch of Royal yearlings were going through their kindergarten stage when we visited with Charles at the helm. The first thing that struck me was the suppleness the youngsters displayed as

Birdcage Walk , 4 years, ridden by Eldred Wilson, first in his Hunter Class at the Royal Norfolk Show before going into training.

The Queen Mother visiting Major and Mrs Eldred Wilson at Harpley Dams for the making of the Central T.V. film, Royal Champion.

he drove them before him by use of long reins. They changed directions at the slightest command from their coach with the ease and willingness of a car with power assisted steering.

The secret is Captain Radclyffe does not break a horse's wild spirit whilst going through the alarming process of getting a horse to accept a rider on his back when previously they have only looked humans in the eye.

"They are like children, do you see", he explains. "It is just the same for them as it was for me in school. Instead of an hour's work, once a day, I prefer to take young horses out five or six times for ten minute lessons. One long teach in tends to tire them and they start to resist and when doing that you have to battle with them. I like them to enjoy what they are doing while learning at the same time."

Times have changed in many ways with a greater emphasis on a quick turn around among new owners. Thankfully, the Royal inmates are allowed all the time they need for Charles Radclyffe to do the job he has been sent the horses for, to make their mouths receptive to the commands of their riders so that trainers and jockeys can do their job.

Recently, a flat trainer sent a horse to Lew House to be schooled for hurdles adding that Charles could take as long as he needed provided it was within three days!!

Of the three 1994 yearlings to go through his hands, one got a "I'm mad for this horse" and the others a "Good Heavens, Good Lord." Horses do change as they develop but Queen Elizabeth has a nice crop from 1992 and some exciting last year's foals, and by the time this record is published the mares will be scraping their straw bedding into a pile in preparation for another crop of foals. Will we see a Gold Cup contender among them when their chance comes in the year 2003?

Chapter 16

A Late Exposure,
Bernard Parkin: Photographer
by Royal Appointment

Bernard Parkin is responsible for the majority of the photographs in this record of Queen Elizabeth's racing life starting as long ago as 1953 and although asked to contribute to the Royal racing records for the past 32 years, has only been the holder of a Royal Warrant for three of them.

"I suppose it was my own naivety, it was only by chance someone happened to mention that tradesmen apply for the warrant, it is not given as an honour would be in The Queen's Birthday list. But then I had been capturing The Queen Mother on film for forty years for pleasure as well as part of my work, that in itself was reward enough."

Born in Cheltenham 65 years ago (he looks fifty). Bernard learned to ride in his early teens and progressed to riding in gallops for the then numerous trainers based around Cleeve Hill.

The nearest he ever got to race riding though came at Woodmancote annual fete where from 1951 to 55 the aspiring jockey finished second three times in the Cart Horse Derby. These events were the highlight of all the fund raising ploys with fierce competition and frighteningly heavy betting.

I was only seven when they held the first of these novel events and can still see the toothless grin of the champion 'Goggy' Jones. As consistent as Bernard Parkin proved, he could never beat Goggy who clung to these great animals' backs as if he were its skin.

Most weighed a ton, none wore a saddle, there were no railings to keep them on the course and the enthusiasm of the riders was only outdone by that of the large crowds they drew. Not too surprising I suppose, the Cart Horse Derbys were halted by the R.S.P.C.A., who considered it to be cruel to the horses (they'd never had such fun in their lives) and by the local police force who thought it to be dangerous, which if we are honest, it was.

Even so the Prestbury Church Bells were re-hung as a direct result of Bernard and his co madmen's exploits. If you happen to catch a peel or two when you're queueing for entrance to the racecourse, perhaps you will look at the Royal Racing Photographer with a slightly altered view.

Photography crept into the act during National Service when serving under Colonel Frank Weldon, of later Badminton Three day Event fame and Lord Mountbatten when at sea. Both men kept Polo Ponies which fired Parkin's artistic imagination, already bent on drawing and all forms of art work including his renowned caricatures.

After his two year stint in the army, Bernard joined a small Cheltenham based firm of engineers Spirax-Sarco as their in house artist and has spent the subsequent 46 years at that post until retiring in 1991.

Bernard thinks his artistic eye prompted the aptitude for taking interesting photographs as he had no training in that area.

It was then and still is now, quite unusual for a business to employ an artist purely to enlighten the work-force. The founder, Brian Northcott, believed the firm should grow as a family and decided to keep everyone in touch via a monthly magazine. The company's artist soon showed an aptitude for cartoons and caricatures and that job continued to be Bernard's even when the energy conservation business became worldwide. The day job dovetailed nicely with his growing passion for racing photography moulding a rare person, a contented man.

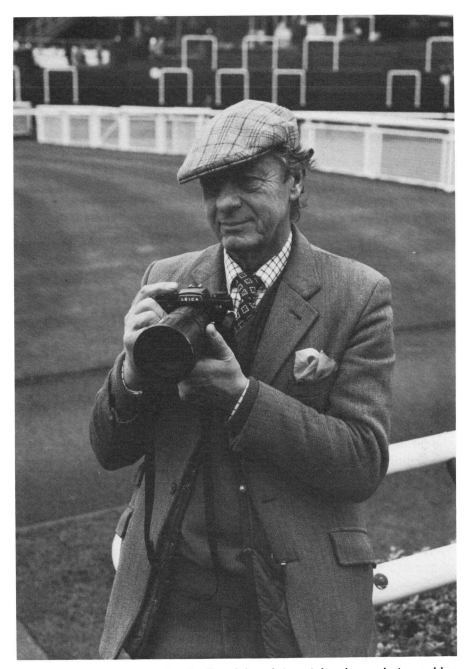

Bernard Parkin, Photographer by Royal Appointment, has been photographing the Queen Mother for 4 decades. *(Charles Parkin)*

"My dark room was the bath for a good many years, all the pictures would be floating in the bath filled with developing solution and I'd be working until 2 am. On Sunday mornings, after only a couple of hours sleep, the day was taken up with packaging the results off to winning owners and jockeys in the hope they'd order enough to have covered the previous day's costs."

Not wanting to lose either his artists or photography jobs, Bernard managed to keep them apart and also not wishing to get under the feet of the daily press, usually took his shots a fence or two from home, a ploy that has become the norm these days.

"I clearly remember taking a low angle shot of you", he told me. "You said I must be mad to be taking shots so close to the horses hooves. Four minutes later they brought you back to the stands in an ambulance and I remember thinking perhaps I'd got the safer job after all!", the Royal photographer reminisced.

"You do have to keep one eye looking behind you though, as funny things happen on the racecourse, loose horses come from the most unexpected places. I'm also very careful to observe the rules, although that is not the case with everyone in the search for the one picture that proves head and shoulders above the others. You quite often see over ambitious snappers firing off shots through the wing of a fence which is quite likely to distract a horse at the crucial moment when deciding where to take off."

If Bernard does play to the rules his work has not suffered as a result with a string of awards to his name.

Soon after being called up for National Service Bernard obtained his first close sighting of Queen Elizabeth, who in 1948 attended the Army Cup Final at Aldershot with The King. Half way through the match lightening struck the referee's metal whistle, paralysing him. The bolt bounced off the instrument only to kill a player and knocking a whole lot more to the ground including the 18 year old Parkin and other spectators who were within a certain radius. The King ordered the game to be abandoned and as a direct result metal whistles were replaced by the modern plastic version.

Parkin vividly remembers his next sight of the Queen Mother when living in Newbarn Lane in Prestbury, part of the Royal route to the racecourse. The shy demobbed soldier had the satisfaction of receiving a return wave from the then Queen. Little did he suspect he'd be invited to various Royal functions later in life through the merit of his photographic career .

In 1953 Bernard was still using his simple box Brownie to take photo's for his own amusement as well as for The Sporting Life and Horse and Hound. Having taken a position at Cheltenham's third last jump away from the crowds at the final fence, Bernard looked up to see Queen Elizabeth roaring towards him standing on the open back of a Land Rover as she tracked her horse Monaveen at close quarters. No electronic tractor driven cameras then, a solitary take was all Bernard Parkin could snatch coincidently exactly the same task facing the horses doing battle at the jump beside him.

It worked, his instincts reacted like a good game shooter's gun when surprised by a lone pheasant. Bernard and his Brownie locked onto the Royal racegoer as she sped by and the result of that frozen moment is testament to the young photographer's skill.

Forty one years and a lot of celluloid through his camera, Bernard was commissioned to take a series of photographs of Queen Elizabeth and her 400th winner Nearco Bay specifically for the 1994 Royal Christmas Card. November 2nd was the only date that the task could be completed due to The Queen Mother's packed engagement schedule and as the venue was to be the Lambourn gallops followed by a tour of Nicky Henderson's stables, the smile of good fortune from the weather was paramount.

The sun shone all right and judging by the poor conditions either side of the chosen day, the gamble had come off. Bernard admits to being somewhat nervous and was glad he had not known of the commission before he and his wife Pam flew away on a fortnight's holiday in the sun in October. "I would have worried the whole time we were away and not slept a wink. You see because there could only be one take, everything had to slot into place, they so wanted this particular shot for the 1994 Christmas card and at that time of year either driving rain or the low cloud that can envelope the Downs, could have meant a total abandonment of the plan.

When I wrote to Michael Oswald to accept the invitation I told him he'd picked the correct day as it coincided with All Saints Day. I hoped the saints would be smiling upon us and they certainly did.

Everything came together, all I had to do was position the horse, trainer and owner correctly, ensure the composition of the background fitted in, check I had a film in the camera (Oh yes, it has been known for the best of photographers to forget the most obvious) correct the exposure and attempt to quell the nerves.

In retrospect it was always going to work unless something silly interjected."

Consider the scenario, The Queen Mother wearing her customary high heeled shoes posing with a highly fit racehorse on winter soft ground with a south westerly wind blowing under his tail. Worse still the Queen Mother had her right leg heavily bandaged due to a holiday accident which had forced her to miss the laying of the wreaths at The Cenotaph.

Many a sound thirty year old horse owner has found it difficult to maintain balance when walking across the gallops, let alone someone of 94. Yet again Queen Elizabeth proved more than up to the task which went off without even so much as a held breath from her aids, none of whom could be near enough to offer help had it been needed as they had to keep out of shot.

Now, as over the past 46 years while owning thoroughbreds, Queen Elizabeth stubbornly resists any steadying help. She has always been a hands on owner, enjoying contact rather than praising from afar. It is my sincerest wish that Queen Elizabeth starts to accept a guiding arm in her 95th year. If you were to fall in the Parade ring or winner's enclosure Ma'am, half the racegoers present would probably die of a heart attack for fear of your own health.

I digress though, back to the start of Royal Photographer Bernard Parkin's tale. It proved another 8 years after the fortuitous Land Rover photo at Cheltenham before a further link was forged with The Queen Mother.

Bernard took a routine shot of Queen Elizabeth's handsome and useful Double Star when the chaser narrowly missed out on victory at a Worcester meeting in 1961. Sir Norman Gwatkin, Controller, Lord Chamberlain's Office, requested him to supply any future photographs of her horses to Clarence House for inclusion in the Royal Racing Records. Thirty four years later that task continues.

"The first specific commission centred around the Cheltenham Gold Cup and Game Spirit, Her Majesty's self confessed favourite chaser. He had Terry Biddlecombe in the saddle, who rated very highly among

Queen Elizabeth's jockeys and top of my own heroes. Terry came out top for me due to his natural ability in the saddle and flair that few of his rivals ever got near to attaining. His personality shone through and transmitted to his horses who seemed to raise their game for him. Terry and Game Spirit were a matched pair.

My brief was to get an action shot should the horse get into the first three places and as he was considered a doubtful stayer, the commission looked very much in jeopardy.

Terry Biddlecombe on the day he retired from the saddle, after coming third in the Cheltenham Gold Cup on Game Spirit. This picture was commissioned by The Queen Mother, should her horse be placed. March 1974. *(Bernard Parkin)*

As it happened when Pendil was brought down at the third last fence it allowed Game Spirit to hang onto the vital third place and the commission went ahead. The shot of Queen Elizabeth sharing the thrill of the race with Terry in the unsaddling enclosure immediately afterwards, remains one of my own personal favourite moments.

It was at Cheltenham later that same day when Terry retired from the saddle. The spontaneous vocal reception from the crowd as he rode onto the course for the last time, literally bounced down the course in waves to engulf me as well, it remains one of those magical moments frozen in time."

Other Royal commissions followed from The Queen Mother, The Princess Royal and Prince Charles. Several of these are displayed in Clarence House as well as a cartoon Bernard created to celebrate Queen Elizabeth's 80th birthday. This depicted a jockey in Her Majesty's racing silks standing on the running rails conducting a group of horses singing "Happy Birthday Ma'am".

It did occur to Bernard that perhaps Sir Martin Gilliat fetched his work out specifically whenever the artist had cause to visit but he is adamant that they were permanently on view.

Another situation that reflects Parkin's position as a Royal Warrant holder and in his capacity of official photographer to the Cheltenham Steeplechase Company, came in March 1994 when there was a security scare at the Festival after Viking Flagship won The Queen Mother Champion Chase. Mindful of the regard winning owners put on the personal presentation by The Queen Mother, it was decided to carry on as normal on the balcony adjoining the Royal Box in full view of the public. Bernard Parkin was the sole photographer allowed at the presentation although modern day long lenses enabled others to capture the moment as well.

Besides the triumphs, Bernard has also seen the other end of the spectrum steeplechasing inevitably throws up. He was present at Newbury the day Game Spirit died having just finished fourth at his most favoured course. I make no apology for including the emotional photograph because sadly this is another side of steeplechasing, one which Queen Elizabeth shares and feels deeply about like any other racehorse owner.

It has been said that if anyone feels uneasy in Queen Elizabeth's company, she blames herself for not having been able to put them at ease. The same consideration applies to those doing their job of work, Parkin reveals. "The Queen Mother is so helpful to cameramen. She has the ability to appreciate what is required to get a decent picture and when able, positions herself without being asked to do so."

Not unlike in cricket when a batsman is on 99 runs, the last one often proves elusive. So it proved when Queen Elizabeth's 400th drew near. I chased around all over the country determined not to miss out on the one racing historians will always remember. It began to look as if everyone would have to wait until the 1994/5 season then Nicky Henderson pulled the rabbit out of the hat. I could not be happier with the photographic evidence.

A copy of The Queen Mother's 80th birthday Card, which still stands on show in Clarence House 15 years later. Another example of Bernard Parkin's work.

Chapter 17

The Future and the Past intertwine

Queen Elizabeth is currently breeding from four mares, the result of a concerted effort to cull those fillies not up to a certain standard of conformation. It had been five until Caserta had to be put down last year after suffering persistent bouts of colic when she was in great pain.

Michael Oswald considers their offspring are as nice a bunch of horses as any National Hunt owner could hope for and is thoroughly looking forward to them showing their paces in public.

"Queen Elizabeth takes a definite hand in the selection of stallions for matings and has derived a great deal of pleasure from watching the results grow through all stages from foaling to racing. She knows them all as a mother would know her children," the Royal stud and racing manager enthused.

"In all there are fourteen youngsters from this quintet of mares around our various studs and livery yards. Others have that have not matched the standards have been given away and only time will tell if we made the right decisions. All four mares are due to foal in 1995 so the string is growing at quite a pace."

FIRST ROMANCE is the apple of the eye. She won one novice hurdle at Towcester in 1987 as a five year old but her breeding is from

The Queen Mother's 1994 foals at Sandringham. "Look out boys, that lovely lady, who gives us carrots is coming over". *(Mandy Pitman)*

one of the oldest and most successful steeplechasing lines, being out of Roman Meeting an unraced sister to the great Spanish Steps. This mare was a gift to Her Majesty from Edward Courage a great friend of The Queen Mother's.

Her eldest offspring is a 5 year old mare called Bewitch by Idiots Delight, she will be showing her paces soon from Ian Balding's stable. "She resembled a long weak drink for three years but made up nicely from then and I've changed my mind for the better about her" is Michael's comment.

Her 3 year old half brother by Bold Owl is much sharper and will not need so much time. The 1992 foal is also a colt, this one's by Rakaposhi King called King's Rhapsody. Like most of The Queen Mother's youngsters, he winters out in well sheltered paddocks at Raynham. He'll also come to hand quite quickly and will go like his elder half brother to be trained by Nicky Henderson.

Last year First Romance had another colt, this time by our stallion Bustino who is a great favourite of Queen Elizabeth's. This is as nice a foal as we have ever bred, neat and compact, I'll be surprised if he does not grow into a good horse.

First Romance is due to foal this April to Bustino and will visit him again to be covered in May. Mares can be covered when they come into season just four or five days after giving birth, otherwise the next heat would be three weeks later.

CASERTA has left The Queen Mother with a legacy of four foals to keep the mare's memory alive. The eldest is Keel Row in training with Tim Thomson-Jones at Lambourn. She had been placed from a couple of runs in 1994, then won in January 1995 with more to come. The mare was barren in 1991 and produced a filly the next year which was subsequently given away at the yearling stage.

She has a 2 year old colt by Ardross named Easter Ross, he has a big plain head although he grows on me every day. Caserta's last foal is a grey filly by Neltino who is nice with plenty of size.

ROYAL SEAL, who is home bred out of Colonia, never ran herself as she has a clubbed foot. We kept her though because she is so well bred and thankfully has not yet passed that deformity on to any of her four foals.

We gave her first and third fillies away but she has already had a

Trainer, Tim Thomson Jones, greets The Queen Mother at Sandown Park. He trains her home bred, Keel Row, one of the young winners to continue the success story. *(Gerry Cranham)*

The Queen Mother loves to see horses at Sandringham and displays a real rapport with everyone.

runner in Stamp Duty who Nicky Henderson says will win chases. Her two year old by Bustino, Royal Mint, is one of the three colts of that age that are exciting, although I originally thought the least of this one and probably still do but he is catching up.

That is one of the exciting things about breeding, the youngsters continually surprise you and not always for the better.

Royal Seal is due to foal a Bustino in March and will again be covered by him this season.

HIGHLAND LYRIC was in training with Fulke Walwyn, he loved her and even called her 'Darling'.

Her first live foal is now a strapping Pitpan 4 year old we've called Montrose. He's with Charles Radclyffe for final education before joining Nicky Henderson for a couple of runs this year.

We also have a nice big 3 year old filly by Bustino called Close Harmony out of the mare and an even bigger 2 year old Broadsword filly named Maid of Morven who will take and be given plenty of time.

Highland Lyric is the earliest of our mares to foal in January.

The home bred Stamp Duty, John Kavanagh, going out onto the course at Newbury with the new Berkshire Stand in the background. It had been opened that day by The Queen Mother. 28th November 1992. *(Bernard Parkin)*

BRAND is the latest addition to the band of mares Queen Elizabeth is breeding from. She was bred by the Queen and although the only one to have a fault, being back at the knee, is so well related it is worth taking the chance that she will not pass it on.

She has a bay filly foal by Broadsword and is due to drop one by Elmaamul in March.

Brand is out of Beacon Hill who is a full sister to Height of Fashion, probably the best mare at stud in the world as she has bred Nashwan, winner of the 2000 Gns, Derby and Coral Eclipse. We may have been criticised in some areas for selling Height of Fashion, but the price was high and ask yourself if we'd have sent her to be mated with Northern Dancer?"

Michael Oswald celebrated his 25th year as manager of the Royal Studs and Racing manager to The Queen Mother on January 1st 1995 and fits the bill to a tee.

He gained his first insight into the fascinating world of racing while ill at his prep school. His room mate happened to be subsequent trainer Roddy Armytage, father of jockeys Marcus and Gee. With nothing better to do he read Roddy's racing books and found breeding of most interest.

A stint in the Scot's Guards and then The King's Own Royal Regiment preceded a degree course at Cambridge reading History and Economics which in turn led to a job in the City. The latter sat uneasily on Michael Oswald's shoulders prompting him to cajole the likes of Noel Murless, Bill Curling, Bunty Scroope and Peter Burrell to find him a way into the stud world.

Sir Noel Murless came up with the first suggestion when saying "If you're as mad about it as you sound I'll get you a place under Europe's best Stud Groom, Jack Podmore at the MacDonald-Buchanan's Lordship and Egerton Studs in Newmarket. It will be a hard, fair job with no wages but you will learn if you have the desire."

Michael's father was less than amused at having put his son through Cambridge only to see him go off to Newmarket as a groom!

Add to this the fact that Michael and his wife Lady Angela Oswald had a two year old daughter, were living in a tied cottage and was working for nothing as a pupil assistant. Yes, perhaps he did appear bent on a fools errand.

Within three years Michael Oswald had taken over the running of

Lordship and Egerton and had made people sit up and take notice to such effect that Lord Tryon asked him if he would consider the appointment he holds today.

At the time the MacDonald-Buchanan studs had Owen Tudor, Abernant and Acropolis and for a while during the transition period in 1970 Michael overlapped that job with Sandringham, where Ribero held court as the first syndicated stallion.

Richard Shelley who was retiring from the position of Stud Manager and Racing Manager to The Queen through ill health, showed Michael around the Royal Studs at Sandringham and nearby Wolferton plus the leased Polhampton (near Kingsclere in Berkshire), Hampton Court and in Ireland. "At the time I did not know he was so ill, he needed a day in bed to get over the exertions of showing me the studs. That is a true test of character, to go through such pain without ever publicly displaying the discomfort or allowing anyone else to notice the situation. I am indeed indebted to him," Michael reflected.

Now, in his own mind's honour's list, the Royal Studs Manager says of Sandringham's stud groom Barry Lister, "He's as good at his job as Jack Podmore was and that is the first time I have said that in 35 years. He can both practice and preach the business better than any stud groom in the U.K."

Two main changes were made after Michael Oswald took over, the Hampton Court stud ceased for thoroughbreds and the Irish side was run down with the heart of operations transferred to Sandringham. With the troubles starting up in Ireland it took little reasoning to move all horses back to England. This also meant The Queen and The Queen Mother could see far more of their home breds as they grew up and over the past twenty-five years that side of things has given both mother and daughter a much closer bond with their horses. Michael is not purely an observer and decision maker, he is very much an action man, interested in all things military from tanks to ships and possibly a slight preference for aircraft. He has flown alongside pilots in twenty-five different types of Military airplanes from twenty-one units, including squeezing into a Red Arrow Hawk and two trips on Ark Royal. To qualify for the fast jet flights Queen Elizabeth's racing manager has to go on a strict diet as the regulations covering the minimum and maximum weight for the ejector seat to work in such aircraft is strictly adhered to.

Lady Angela Oswald, Lady In Waiting to Her Majesty, The Queen Mother, who could never be accused of being a 'fair weather owner'.

Lady Angela Oswald, the youngest daughter of The Marquess of Exeter, who hunted hounds in East Sussex, The Old Berks and then his own pack at Burghley. He also won a Gold medal at The Helsinki Olympics in 1928 for the high hurdles, then took silver four years later at Los Angeles.

She herself is bred in the purple as her mother was the daughter of The Duke of Buccleuch. She was the least horsey of their children yet has grown into two major roles that encompass racehorses within the Royal Household. As Michael's wife she is involved with the stud and racing activities and as Lady in Waiting to the Queen Mother she has an appointment in her own right.

The latter came about in 1981 as a natural progression having been present with Michael whenever The Queen Mother's horses ran during the preceding eleven years. Being so knowledgeable about racing and its participants Angela Oswald is better equipped than most to serve Queen Elizabeth whose racing activities take up a good portion of the winter leisure time.

Queen Elizabeth has not only maintained her standing among her daughter's subjects but she commands respect from generation after generation of the racing professionals who realise exactly how much she does know about racing as a whole, not just her own horses. 7500 letters arrived on her 94th birthday.

During the early years The Queen Mother listened to racing in the privacy of Clarence House via the Victoria audio system known as 'The Blower', later to become Extel. Since 1990 though she has enjoyed the added dimension of actually seeing the action having subscribed to S.I.S. who, besides supplying live racing of at least two meetings per day, cover anything up to 5 fixtures on Saturdays. Another facet she has come to utilise is their evening service which relays all that afternoon's racing edited together into a continuous package.

Whatever your own thoughts on The Queen Mother's after dinner relaxation, I'll lay 100/1 watching the 2:30 p.m. novice chase from Plumpton did not feature very high on your list?

It has long been The Queen Mother's policy to find alternative uses for her racehorses when their racing days were over through injury or simply because they had earned a less demanding life. Equally she is very sensible and pragmatic. If a horse has something wrong with it that cannot be put right, she will readily agree to put it down if that is the kindest thing to do.

She is also the first to criticise her own horses, never overrating them and rather inclined to say "He's not really very good, is he?", secretly hoping Michael Oswald or the trainer will disagree. She is one of life's great enhancers making racing fun at all times, in no way has she ever made it a business nor gone out to buy success when paying big money for her purchases.

"I have never heard her criticise a jockey although in the days before the whip rule was changed to it's present form, she didn't like to see her horses what she called 'whacked'." Michael observed, "Queen Elizabeth is very much at one with Tim Forster who dislikes hurdle races as horses coming off the flat tend to race too fast over timber. If she had her way jumping would be confined to steeplechases. We set out to breed three mile chasers with the Cheltenham Gold Cup the goal.

She is somewhat nervous in an excited way before a big race and rather wishes the whole thing was over. The Queen Mother is much

Rogues Gallery? No, The Queen Mother's jockeys. Sir Edward Cazalet is centre of the back row , wearing gloves.   *(Bernard Parkin)*

happier going for a modest contest where the day is low key and nothing but fun.

The Queen Mother never bets, although her long time Private Secretary, Sir Martin Gilliat loved to do so. It was an in joke, whenever he backed a loser he'd turn to Queen Elizabeth and say 'Well, there goes the car, we'll have to go home on the bus'.

She has had quality and quantity and derived tremendous enjoyment from following the fortunes of her horses in retirement."

From that first batch of Irish youngsters Gipsy Love found his way to the 9th Lancers for members of the regiment to point to point while another, Flamingo Bay, even failed between the flags for Eldred Wilson but did make a hunter and more.

Major Peter Borwick used the gelding for seven successive seasons as Master's horse with the Pytchley, taking the considerable fences with ease never once falling. During the summer when his contempories were out at grass, Flamingo Bay doubled up as starter's hack at Royal Ascot for Alec Marsh. Queen Elizabeth always made a fuss of her former hurdler, making a point of patting him while waiting in the parade ring.

Brig O'Dee ended up with the Metropolitan Police College at Imber Court and delighted everyone when part of their team giving a musical ride at the Royal Norfolk Horse Show.

Devon Loch spent some time at Warren Place as Noel Murless's hack while the laid back Worcran served the same purpose for The Queen. The handsome chestnut lived out his retirement at Windsor in great comfort where he proved a superb ride for the Sovereign, as did Castle Yard, who had won the Zetland Gold Cup for her before taking three jump races for the Queen Mother.

The home bred Zaloba who won decent staying races on the flat for The Queen, including The Queen's Prize when trained by Sir Cecil Boyd Rochfort, went on to record three hurdle race victories from Fairlawne, amazingly always in January. He became Michael Oswald's ride around the Sandringham Estate in the years when his children were into eventing and well remembers the thrill he only previously imagined jockeys derived from partnering an equine athlete. "Leading off from the stud buildings here the road has a wide verge running for a mile and seven furlongs straight without any interruptions, it's better than many trainer's gallops. Giving five stones away to my children who were on fit horses Zaloba cruised past them effortlessly, it was the most wonderful feeling."

Inch Arran went to Ian Farquhar when he was Master of the Bicester Hunt and although he pulled like crazy on the course and did not settle for Ian, he responded to Ian's wife Pammy-Jane's good hands to become a superb hunter.

His full brother Colonius, who had all of Inch Arran's traits but jumped appallingly every now and then, went to Michael Farrin, the huntsman to the Quorn, where he enjoyed being out front as he'd done all his racing life.

The third prolific winner from that same family was Isle of Man who also saw out his days carrying "the Horn" for Michael Farrin. Like his brother and half brother he was excitable and loved to front run, so being a huntsman's mount suited well. He may not have settled so well for a follower, it is all a question of matching the horse to the right job in retirement. The grey Bel Ambre who managed one victory every year for three consecutive seasons found his way to the 9th Lancers where he taught no end of soldiers to raceride in point to points and Hunter Chases under Jumbo Wilkinson's care at Middleham in North Yorkshire. Not to be seen to favour one of the Forces, Paramount went to R.A.F. Finningly as a schoolmaster for novice eventers.

Many others such as Just Lit, Admiral's Leap, Royal Pavilion, Sun Rising and the ugly duckling, Dudley, all went on permanent loan to girls around the British Isles as hacks or hunters.

Lunedale went north of the border to the country of his owner's birth where Stuart and Asher Nardone get unending pleasure from the gelding riding around the wilds of Banffshire in North East Scotland.

Sunshine Flight is showjumping and has made a promising start.

Special Cargo having proved too boisterous for Henry Cecil has nannied our lame and young stock at Raynham and is still doing so aged twenty two. While the headstrong Master Andrew did adapt to everyday life as a hack for Richard Lancaster and his wife at Sheikh Hamdan al Maktoum's Shadwell Stud where Richard is manager.

Russ Hill stayed closest to home in West Norfolk where farmer and top rider and trainer of point to points, David Wales took him on to hunt. Another currently seen out with The Beaufort and The Tedworth is The Argonaut who has carried Lambourn vet Bobby McEwen since the gelding retired five years ago.

Bobby looked after the New Zealand bred chaser throughout his racing life with Fulke Walwyn and he could not have gone to a better or more loving home. His wife Ali hunts Blythe Tate's former Olympic eventer Tempo, now also in retirement and the couple cut a considerable dash together. Bobby and The Argonaut favour hedges with Tempo and Ali the more stylish over upright rails.

From conception through the growing years to the racecourse and on into active retirement, Queen Elizabeth is wherever her horses are. She regards them as friends, cheers them on to victory and pats them even more in defeat. She feeds them titbits from birth to pension age and asks nothing from them other than to enjoy what they are bred to do. She is herself a kind and gentle person which horses can sense at twenty paces. They are good judges of human nature which is probably why despite being a hands on owner Queen Elizabeth has never been bitten by one of her horses.

Lambourn Vet, Bobby McEwen, on point duty with The Tedworth Hunt, riding The Argonaut in January 1995.

The Future and the Past intertwine

The Winners

MONAVEEN
B.G. 1942 Landscape Hill - Great Double
Trainer: Major P.V. Cazalet (In joint ownership with H.R.H. The Princess Elizabeth)

1949
10th October	Fontwell	Chichester Handicap Chase	Tony Grantham
26th November	Sandown	Walton Green Chase	Tony Grantham
31st December	Hurst Park	QUEEN ELIZABETH CHASE	Tony Grantham

1950
11th February	Hurst Park	George Williamson Handicap Chase	Tony Grantham

MANICOU
B.H. 1945   Last Post - Mylae
Trainer: Major P.V. Cazalet

1950
24th November	Kempton	Wimbledon Handicap Chase	Tony Grantham
14th December	Sandown	Ewell Chase	Bryan Marshall
26th December	Kempton	KING GEORGE VI CHASE	Bryan Marshall

M'AS - TU - VU
Br.G. 1946   Pampeiro - Malle Poste
Trainer: Major P.V. Cazalet

1953
27th November	Kempton	Wimbledon Handicap Chase	Dick Francis
5th December	Lingfield	Blindley Heath Handicap Chase	Dick Francis

1955
22nd January	Newbury	Ogbourne Handicap Chase	Dick Francis
16th March	Lingfield	Sussex Chase	Arthur Freeman
26th November	Lingfield	Eridge Handicap Chase	Dick Francis

1956
14th March	Lingfield	Sussex Chase	Arthur Freeman

DEVON LOCH
Br.G. 1946 Devonian - Coolaleen
Trainer: Major P.V. Cazalet

1955

5th February	Hurst Park	New Century Chase	Bryan Marshall
18th March	Sandown	Beech Open Chase	Bryan Marshall
25th November	Lingfield	Blindley Heath Handicap Chase	Dick Francis
14th December	Sandown	Sandown Handicap Chase	Dick Francis

1956

29th October	Nottingham	Bulcote Hurdle	Dick Francis
13th December	Sandown	Ewell Chase	Dick Francis
26th December	Kempton	2nd, KING GEORGE VI CHASE	Dick Francis

DOUBLE STAR
Br.G 1952 Arctic Star - Bright Star
Trainer: Major P.V. Cazalet

1956

7th December	Lingfield	Caterham Novices' Hurdle	Dick Francis
15th December	Hurst Park	Maze Novices' Hurdle (Div II)	Dick Francis

1957

18th January	Sandown	Metropolitan Novices' Hurdle (Div 1)	Arthur Freeman
26th October	Cheltenham	Nailsworth Handicap Hurdle	Arthur Freeman
22nd November	Sandown	Novices' Steeplechase	Arthur Freeman
30th November	Newbury	Tote Investors Cup Chase	Arthur Freeman

1958

24th October	Newbury	Evenlode Chase	Arthur Freeman
6th December	Lingfield	Ashdown Handicap Chase	Arthur Freeman

1959

8th January	Hurst Park	Star and Garter Handicap Chase	Arthur Freeman
4th February	Hurst Park	Richmond Handicap Chase	Arthur Freeman

1960

9th January	Sandown	Londesborough Handicap Chase	Arthur Freeman
13th February	Sandown	Gainsborough Chase	Arthur Freeman
3rd December	Lingfield	Ashdown Handicap Chase	Bill Rees

1961

9th December	Lingfield	Ashdown Handicap Chase	Bill Rees

1962

27th January	Lingfield	Hidden Mystery Handicap Chase	Bill Rees
22nd March	Lingfield	Limpsfield Handicap Chase	Bill Rees

1963

9th March	Newbury	Paddington Handicap Chase	Bill Rees

The Winners

KING'S POINT
Ch.G. 1949 Queens's Eyot - Steel Girl
Trainer: Major P.V. Cazalet

1957
12th January   Newbury   Newtown Maiden Hurdle (Div 1)   Arthur Freeman

1958
22nd February   Sandown   Kingston Handicap Hurdle   Arthur Freeman

WILD WEST
Ch.G. 1951 Mustang - Blissful
Trainer: Major P.V. Cazalet

1957
10th September   Folkestone   Channel Tunnel Novices' Hurdle   Arthur Freeman

KING OF THE ISLE
Ch. or Br.G. 1951 King Hal - G.B.R.
Trainer: Major P.V. Cazalet

1958
8th March   Newbury   Whatcombe Maiden Hurdle (Div. I)   Arthur Freeman

1960
23rd January   Kempton   Staines Handicap Hurdle   David Mould

SPARKLING KNIGHT
B.G. 1952 Cameron - Sparkling Gold
Trainer: Major P.V. Cazalet

1958
18th October   Worcester   St Barnabas Handicap Chase   Arthur Freeman
13th December   Windsor   BuckinghamshireHandicap Chase   Arthur Freeman

1959
8th January   Hurst Park   Tolworth Handicap Chase   Arthur Freeman

OUT OF TOWN
B.G. 1954 Owenstown - Dismissal
Trainer: Major P.V. Cazalet

1959
9th January   Newbury   Newton Hurdle (Div. II)   Arthur Freeman
12th February   Newbury   Compton Novices' Hurdle (Div II)   Arthur Freeman

1961

25th September	Folkestone	Broadstairs Chase	Bill Rees
22nd November	Kempton	Wimbledon Handicap Chase	Bill Rees
8th December	Lingfield	Blindley Heath Handicap Chase	Bill Rees

1963

25th September	Folkestone	Whitelaw Gold Cup Handicap Chase	David Mould
5th November	Folkestone	Canterbury Handicap Chase	David Mould

INQUISITIVE PETE
Ch.G. 1952 Grand Inquisitor - Duchess of Pedulus
Trainer: Major P.V. Cazalet

1960

28th March	Fontwell	March Novices' Chase (Div. II)	Arthur Freeman
7th November	Fontwell	Cissbury Handicap Chase	Bill Rees

GAY RECORD
B.G.1952 Archive - Merryland
Trainer: J. O'Donoghue

1960

15th October	Fontwell	Emsworth Novices' Chase	Johnny Lehane

1961

17th November	Sandown	Withington Stayers Handicap Chase	Gene Kelly

1962

3rd February	Windsor	Herne the Hunter Handicap Chase	Gene Kelly
1st March	Windsor	Runnymede Handicap Chase	Gene Kelly

1963

3rd May	Fontwell	Bognor Handicap Chase	Gene Kelly
9th November	Sandown	Walton Green Handicap Chase	Gene Kelly

1964

20th October	Folkestone	Sevenoaks Handicap Chase	Bobby Beasley
4th November	Folkestone	Canterbury Handicap Chase	Bobby Beasley

1966

24th October	Wye	East Kent Handicap Chase	Michael Scudamore

SILVER DOME
Ch.G. 1954 Domaha - Silverina
Trainer: Major P.V. Cazalet

1961

14th January	Sandown	Londesborough Handicap Chase	Bill Rees
7th December	Sandown	Palace Handicap Chase	Bill Rees

1962

3rd March	Kempton	Portlane Handicap Chase	Bill Rees
9th November	Sandown	Littleworth Handicap Chase	Bill Rees

1963

30th September	Wye	Wye Handicap Chase	Bill Rees

1964

24th January	Kempton	Fulwell Handicap Chase	Willie Powell
30th October	Liverpool	BECHER CHASE	Bill Rees

THE RIP
B.G. 1955 Manicou - Easy Virtue
Trainer: Major P.V. Cazalet

1960

17th October	Hurst Park	Mayflower Novices' Hurdle (Div II)	Bill Rees
25th October	Nottingham	Bulwell Chase	Bill Rees
23rd November	Kempton	Middlesex Novices' Chase	Bill Rees

1961

24th April	Folkestone	Fremlins "Elephant" Handicap Chase	David Mould
18th October	Hurst Park	Grand Sefton Trial Handicap Chase	David Mould
8th November	Newbury	Streatley Handicap Chase	David Mould
23rd November	Kempton	Cottage Rake Handicap Chase	Bill Rees
9th December	Lingfield	Eridge Handicap Chase	Bill Rees

1962

17th February	Hurst Park	Morden Handicap Chase	Bill Rees

1964

16th January	Lingfield	Westerham Handicap Chase	Bill Rees
5th November	Newbury	3rd, HENNESSEY GOLD CUP	Bill Rees

1965

5th February	Kempton	Walter Hyde Handicap Chase	Bill Rees
13th March	Kempton	Coventry Handicap Chase	Dave Dick

1966

31st October	Plumpton	Newhaven Handicap Chase	David Mould

JAIPUR
B.G. 1956 Bois Roussel - Ynys
Trainer: Major P.V. Cazalet

1960

31st October	Birmingham	Bonfire Novices' Hurdle (Div I)	Bill Rees
2nd December	Lingfield	Caterham Novices' Hurdle (Div. II)	Bill Rees

1961
17th November   Sandown   Novices' Chase   Bill Rees

YOUNG RAJAH
Gr.G. 1955 Rajah II - Belle Bailey
Trainer: Major P.V. Cazalet

1962
20th January   Newbury   Wantage Novices' Chase   Bob McCreery

LAFFY
B.G. 1956 Rigolo - Vatelinde
Trainer: Major P.V. Cazalet

1961
9th December   Lingfield   Oxted Novices' Chase (Div. II)   Bill Rees

1962
17th February   Hurst Park   New Century Chase   Bill Rees
22nd March   Lingfield   Tandridge Court Handicap Chase   Bill Rees
6th April   DownPatrick   Ulster Harp National Handicap Chase   Willie Robinson

1963
7th December   Lingfield   Eridge Handicap Chase   David Mould

1964
22nd February   Lingfield   Manifesto Chase   David Mould
25th April   Sandown   3rd, WHITBREAD GOLD CUP   Bill Rees
24th October   Newbury   Capital and Counties Handicap Chase   Bill Rees
19th December   Lingfield   Mountfield Handicap Chase   Bill Rees

1965
27th February   Lingfield   Manifesto Handicap Chase   Dave Dick
17th March   Lingfield   Sussex Handicap Chase   Bill Rees

1966
9th March   Lingfield   Sussex Handicap Chase   David Mould

1967
8th March   Lingfield   Sussex Handicap Chase   David Mould

DARGENT
B.G. 1956 Domaha - Silverina
Trainer: P.V. Cazalet

1962
26th January   Lingfield   Edenbridge Handicap Hurdle   Bill Rees

The Winners

AUGUSTINE
Ch.G. 1957 Aureole - Young Entry
Trainer: T. Masson

1962
9th February   Sandown   Wavendon Handicap Hurdle   Bill Rees

SUPER FOX
B.G. 1957 Supertello - Foxy Jane
Trainer: Major P.V. Cazalet

1962
9th November   Sandown   Waterloo Novices' Hurdle (Div. I)   David Mould

1963
15th April   Plumpton   John Hare Handicap Hurdle   Clive Chapman
25th September   Folkestone   Margate Handicap Hurdle   David Mould
9th October   Worcester   Abberley Handicap Hurdle   David Mould
14th December   Sandown   December Handicap Hurdle   David Mould

1964
11th January   Sandown   Cardinal Handicap Hurdle   David Mould
4th November   Folkestone   Chilham Novices' Chase   David Mould
28th November   Lingfield   Oxted Novices' Chase   Bill Rees

MAKALDAR
Ch.G. 1960 Makalu - La Madouna
Trainer: Major P.V. Cazalet

1963
9th November   Sandown   Toll House Juvenile Hurdle   David Mould
21st November   Kempton   Juvenile Hurdle   David Mould
7th December   Lingfield   Juvenile Hurdle   David Mould
30th December   Fontwell   Worthing Three Years Old Hurdle (Div I)   David Mould

1964
11th January   Sandown   Village Four Year Olds Hurdle   David Mould
7th March   Haydock   VICTOR LUDORUM HURDLE   David Mould
9th December   Sandown   Morningside Hurdle (Div I)   Bill Rees

1965
19th February   Newbury   Stroud Green Handicap Hurdle   Bill Rees
6th May   Newbury   Witney Handicap Hurdle   Bill Rees
18th October   Folkestone   Martin Walter Dormabile Handicap Hurdle   David Mould
13th November   Cheltenham   MACKESON HANDICAP HURDLE   David Mould

1966
29th October   Cheltenham   T.W.W. Hurdle   David Mould

1967
3rd March	Newbury	Eastleigh Handicap Hurdle	David Mould
10th March	Cheltenham	2nd, CHAMPION HURDLE	David Mould
18th November	Ascot	BLACK AND WHITE GOLD CUP CHASE	David Mould

1970
| 3rd January | Sandown | Londesborough Handicap Chase | David Mould |

ANTIAR
B.G. 1958   Antares - V. Day II
Trainer: Major P.V. Cazalet

1965
11th March	Cheltenham	SPA HURDLE	Dave Dick
19th March	Sandown	Beech Open Chase	Bill Rees
31st March	Sandown	Novices' Chase	Bill Rees

1969
| 25th January | Windsor | Caversham Handicap Chase | Richard Dennard |
| 26th February | Windsor | Magna Carta Handicap Chase | Richard Dennard |

WORCRAN
Ch.H. 1958   Worden II - Craneuse
Trainer: Major P.V. Cazalet

1965
23rd February	Birmingham	Elmdon Hurdle (Div. II)	Bobby Beasley
10th March	Cheltenham	3rd, CHAMPION HURDLE	David Nicholson
7th May	Taunton	Melody Man Trophy Hurdle	Bill Rees

BALLYKINE
Ch.G. 1959   Roi de Navarre II - Flowery Path
Trainer: Major P.V. Cazalet

1965
| 22nd February | Birmingham | Graveley Hurdle (Div. III) | Dave Dick |

1966
28th September	Folkestone	Seabrook Handicap Hurdle	David Mould
3rd October	Wye	Tonbridge Handicap Hurdle	David Mould
19th October	Sandown	Heather Novices' Chase	David Mould
5th November	Sandown	November Novices' Chase	David Mould

1968
| 2nd October | Fontwell | Avisford Handicap Chase | David Mould |

The Winners

MEL
Ch.G. 1959 Manicou - Sweeter and Sweeter
Trainer: Major P.V. Cazalet

1964

2nd November	Birmingham	Charlecote Novices' Chase	Willie Powell
23rd November	Folkestone	Channel Tunnel Novices' Chase	Bill Rees

1965

26th February	Lingfield	Old Mill Handicap Chase	David Nicholson

ARCH POINT
B.G. 1960 Archive - Sol Point
Trainer: Major P.V. Cazalet

1964

4th November	Folkestone	Marden Novices' Hurdle (Div. I)	Bill Rees
11th November	Fontwell	Ferring Novices' Hurdle (Div. II)	Bill Rees
27th November	Lingfield	Caterham Novices' Hurdle (Div. I)	Bill Rees

1965

26th February	Lingfield	Sevenoaks Novices' Chase (Div II)	David Nicholson

1967

25th March	Plumpton	Bob Wigney Handicap Hurdle	David Mould
2nd May	Plumpton	Long Distance Handicap Hurdle	David Mould

IRISH ROVER
Ch.G. 1960 Star Signal or Vulgan - Random Inn
Trainer: Major P.V. Cazalet

1965

18th October	Folkestone	Penshurst Novices' Hurdle (Div. II)	Bill Rees
8th November	Folkestone	Maiden Novices' Hurdle (Div. I)	Bill Rees
22nd November	Folkestone	Channel Tunnel Novices' Chase	Bill Rees

1966

4th February	Kempton	Hampton Handicap Chase	David Mould
18th October	Folkestone	Littlestone Handicap Chase	David Mould
17th December	Sandown	Henry VIII Chase	David Mould

1967

14th January	Newbury	Marlborough Handicap Chase	David Mould

BEL AMBRE
Gr.H. 1961 Amber X - Belle Gitane
Trainer: Major P.V. Cazalet

1965
5th November   Sandown   Waterloo Novices' Hurdle (Div. I)   David Mould

1966
9th March   Lingfield   South Eastern Handicap Hurdle   David Mould

1967
20th November   Windsor   White Hart Handicap Hurdle (Div. I)   David Mould

LOCHMORE
B.G. 1961 Mustang - Loch May
Trainer: Major P.V. Cazalet

1965
19th November   Ascot   Bingley Novices' Hurdle (Div. I)   Bill Rees
3rd December   Lingfield   Caterham Novices' Hurdle (Div. I)   Bill Rees

OEDIPE
Br.G. 1958 Foxlight - Ondee de Fleurs
Trainer: Major P.V. Cazalet

1966
29th January   Windsor   Royal Windsor Centenary Chase   David Mould
29th October   Cheltenham   Pratt and Co. Handicap Chase   Mr Nick Gaselee

1967
1st March   Windsor   Runnymede Handicap Chase   Bill Rees

1969
11th January   Newbury   Weyhill Handicap Chase   David Mould

CHARLOT
Br.G. 1963 Doutelle - Nicola
Trainer: Major P.V. Cazalet

1966
5th November   Sandown   Toll House Hurdle (Div. I)   David Mould

1967
3rd March   Newbury   March Hare Handicap Hurdle   David Mould

1968
30th January   Fontwell   Aquarius Handicap Hurdle (Div. II)   David Mould
8th March   Newbury   Eastleigh Handicap Hurdle   David Mould

The Winners

1969
8th January   Windsor   Montem Novices' Chase   David Mould

HIBISCUS
B. or Br.G. 1962   Tangle - Gay Flower
Trainer: P.V. Cazalet

1966
16th December   Sandown   Regent Novices' Hurdle (Div. II)   David Mould

Trainer: J. McMurchie
1970
9th March   Ayr   Hollybush Novices' Chase   Brian Fletcher

CHAOU II
Br. or Gr.G. 1963   Marino - Djanet
Trainer: P.V. Cazalet

1967
22nd March   Folkestone   Four Year Old Hurdle   David Mould
6th April   Liverpool   Lancashire Hurdle   David Mould

1968
6th January   Sandown   Stand Novices' Chase (Div. II)   David Mould
3rd February   Kempton   Weybridge Novices' Chase (Div. I)   David Mould
28th February   Windsor   Magna Carta Handicap Chase   David Mould
18th October   Kempton   Gregalach Handicap Chase   Richard Dennard
26th October   Newbury   Sports Medicine Chase   David Mould
7th November   Newbury   Bagnor Chase   Richard Dennard

1969
10th January   Newbury   Newbury January Handicap Chase   David Mould
15th March   Kempton   Portlane Handicap Chase   David Mould
5th November   Newbury   Bagnor Chase   David Mould

1970
23rd March   Folkestone   Rye Handicap Chase   David Mould
8th April   Worcester   Worcester Royal Porcelain Handicap Chase   David Mould
11th November   Windsor   Royal Lodge Handicap Chase   David Mould

1971
30th January   Kempton   Walter Hyde Handicap Chase   Richard Dennard

1972
22nd November   Fontwell   Whitelaw Challenge Cup Handicap Chase   David Mould
1st December   Kempton   Ewell Handicap Chase   David Mould

RETZ
B.G. 1963 Franc Luron - Redite
Trainer: Major P.V. Cazalet

1967

17th March	Sandown	Select Four Year Old Hurdle	David Mould

1969

28th February	Kempton	Manor Novices' Chase	David Mould

1971

3rd March	Lingfield	Medway Handicap Hurdle	Richard Dennard

WOODMAN
Br.G. 1962 Woodcut - Kirghiz
Trainer: Major P.V. Cazalet

1967

16th November	Plumpton	Chailey Novices' Hurdle	David Mould

1968

28th February	Windsor	Langley Handicap Hurdle	David Mould
9th April	Folkestone	Eastbourne Handicap Hurdle	Richard Dennard
14th October	Folkestone	Chilham Novices' Chase	David Mould
5th November	Folkestone	Channel Tunnel Novices' Chase	David Mould

ESCALUS
B.H. 1965 Lord Of Verona - Singing Hinny
Trainer: Major P.V. Cazalet

1968

5th November	Folkestone	November Hurdle (Div. II)	David Mould
9th November	Sandown	Toll House Hurdle (Div. II)	Richard Dennard
7th December	Lingfield	Juvenile Hurdle (Div. II)	David Mould

1969

1st February	Folkestone	Walton Hurdle	David Mould
28th October	Nottingham	Bulwell Hurdle	David Mould
8th November	Sandown	Ackermann Skeaping Trophy Hurdle	David Mould
13th December	Sandown	Gold Bond Hurdle	Richard Dennard
20th December	Ascot	Copper Horse Hurdle	Richard Dennard

1970

2nd March	Wye	Deal Hurdle	David Mould
18th March	Cheltenham	3rd, CHAMPION HURDLE	David Mould

STUBBS
CH.H. 1964 Preciptic - Bay Fairy
Trainer: Major P.V. Cazalet

1968
6th November   Newbury   Cold Ash Novices' Hurdle (Div. I)   David Mould

1969
22nd March   Lingfield   South Eastern Handicap Hurdle (Div. II)   David Mould

1970
28th March   Plumpton   Bob Wigney Handicap Hurdle   David Mould

NEWBOROUGH
B.G. 1964 New Brig - Smile
Trainer: Major P.V. Cazalet

1968
14th October   Folkestone   Marden Novices' Hurdle (Div. I)   Richard Dennard

1969
24th March   Folkestone   Hastings Novices' Chase   David Mould

1971
3rd February   Windsor   Oakside Handicap Chase   Richard Dennard

THREE NO TRUMPS
B.G. 1959 Richard Louis - Gay Romance
Trainer: Major P.V. Cazalet

1968
23rd October   Sandown   More Lane Handicap Chase   David Mould

STEEL DRUM
B. G. 1965 Pandofell - Tommie
Trainer: Major P.V. Cazalet

1970
30th March   Plumpton   Hailsham Novices' Hurdle (Div. II)   David Mould

ZALOBA
B.G. 1962 Zarathustra - Alesia
Trainer: Major P.V. Cazalet

1970
| 23rd January | Fontwell | Pulborough Novices' Hurdle (Div. II) | David Mould |
| 28th January | Plumpon | Crowborough Novices' Hurdle (Div. I) | David Mould |

1971
| 25th January | Folkestone | Robertsbridge Handicap Hurdle | Richard Dennard |

INCH ARRAN
B.G. 1964   Colonist II - Queen of the Isle
Trainer: Major P.V. Cazalet

1969
| 22nd October | Sandown | Mitre Novices' Chase | Richard Dennard |
| 7th November | Sandown | November Novices' Chase | Richard Dennard |

1970
22nd September	Plumpton	South Downs Handicap Chase	Richard Dennard
5th October	Wye	Wye Handicap Chase	Richard Dennard
6th November	Sandown	Pirbright Handicap Chase	Richard Dennard
30th November	Windsor	Round Oak Handicap Chase	Richard Dennard
19th December	Ascot	"Dunkirk" Handicap Chase	Richard Dennard

1971
| 20th January | Windsor | Castle Handicap Chase | Richard Dennard |
| 4th November | Newbury | Winterbourne Handicap Chase | Richard Dennard |

1972
24th April	Folkestone	Kent Amateur Riders' Handicap Chase	David Evatt
28th October	Liverpool	B. P. Chase	Richard Dennard
27th December	Kempton	Christmas Handicap Chase	Richard Dennard

1973
| 29th March | Liverpool | Topham Trophy Handicap Chase | Richard Dennard |

Trainer: F. Walwyn
1974
| 17th April | Cheltenham | Gratwicke Blagrave Memorial Challenge Cup Handicap Chase | Bill Smith |

CASTLE YARD
B.G. 1963 St. Paddy - Spanish Court
Trainer: Major P.V. Cazalet

1969
| 26th November | Fontwell | Middleton Novices' Hurdle (Div. I) | David Mould |

5th December	Lingfield	Caterham Novices' Hurdle (Div. II)	Richard Dennard
1971			
24th March	Plumpton	Barcombe Novices' Chase (Div. I)	Richard Dennard

BLACK MAGIC
B.G. 1964   Black Tarquin - Ballyrory
Trainer: Major P.V. Cazalet

1969			
20th November	Kempton	Vauxhall Novices' Hurdle (Div. I)	Richard Dennard
1970			
2nd November	Folkestone	Wadhurst Novices' Chase	Richard Dennard
23rd November	Folkestone	Herstmonceux Handicap Chase	Richard Dennard
1971			
1st January	Sandown	Mole Handicap Chase	Richard Dennard
16th January	Ascot	Mar Lodge Handicap Chase	Richard Dennard
6th February	Sandown	Scilly Isles Beginners' Chase	Richard Dennard
6th November	Sandown	SANDOWN PARK PATTERN CHASE	Richard Dennard

MASTER DANIEL
B.G. 1965   Night Life - Avanti
Trainer: Major P.V. Cazalet

1969			
3rd December	Worcester	Hindlip Novices' Hurdle	Richard Dennard
1970			
30th January	Kempton	Woking Handicap Hurdle	Richard Dennard
28th February	Kempton	Rendlesham Handicap Hurdle	Richard Dennard
14th September	Folkestone	Romney Marsh Handicap Hurdle	Richard Dennard
21st September	Folkestone	Tonbridge Novices' Chase	Richard Dennard

COLONSAY ISLE
Gr.G. 1964   Colonist II - Queen of the Sea
Trainer: Major P.V. Cazalet

1970			
10th November	Plumpton	Beacon Novices' Chase	Richard Dennard
24th November	Lingfield	Wilderwick Chase	Richard Dennard

GAME SPIRIT
Ch.G. 1966   Romany Air or Game Rights - Castile
Trainer: Major P.V. Cazalet

1971

12th March	Sandown	Lilac Novices' Hurdle (Div. II)	David Mould
27th March	Newbury	Alvescot Novices' Hurdle (Div. II)	David Mould
5th November	Sandown	November Novices' Chase	David Mould

1972

12th February	Newbury	Compton Chase	David Mould
2nd March	Lingfield	Felcourt Handicap Chase	David Mould
11th March	Sandown	Beech Open Chase	David Mould

1973

13th January	Ascot	Jock Scott Handicap Chase	David Mould
20th January	Windsor	Royal Windsor Handicap Chase	David Mould
28th February	Lingfield	Hidden Mystery Handicap Chase	David Mould
19th March	Folkestone	Whitbread Fremlins "Elephant" Handicap Chase	David Mould
24th March	Newbury	Kencot Handicap Chase	David Mould

Trainer: F. Walwyn

23rd November	Newbury	Clanfield Handicap Chase	Aly Branford
29th December	Newbury	Weyhill Handicap Chase	Terry Biddlecombe

1974

31st January	Wincanton	Wincanton Challenge Cup Chase	Terry Biddlecombe
20th February	Windsor	Fairlawne Chase	Terry Biddlecombe
14th March	Cheltenham	3rd, GOLD CUP	Terry Biddlecombe

1975

1st March	Newbury	Geoffrey Gilbey Memorial Handicap Chase	Bill Smith
10th April	Ascot	Sardan Handicap Chase	Bill Smith
25th October	Newbury	Hermitage Chase	Bill Smith

1976

13th February	Newbury	Thatcham Handicap Chase	Bill Smith
16th March	Cheltenham	2nd, TWO MILE CHAMPION CHASE	Bill Smith
14th April	Ascot	Sardan Handicap Chase	Bill Smith
23rd October	Newbury	Hermitage Chase	Bill Smith

GREYSTOKE PILLAR
Ch.G. 1968   Straight Cut - Residence
Trainer: Major P.V. Cazalet

1972

2nd March	Lingfield	Worth Wood Hurdle (Div. I)	David Mould
17th March	Lingfield	Newleaf Novices' Hurdle (Div. I)	David Mould
22nd November	Fontwell	Brighton Handicap Hurdle	David Mould

Trainer: F. Walwyn

1974			
11th April	Ludlow	Weston Novices' Chase	Aly Branford
22nd April	Fontwell	Flansham Novices' Chase	Aly Branford

1975			
19th February	Windsor	Langley Handicap Hurdle	Bill Smith

KELSO BRIG
B.G. 1968 New Brig - Coin Box
Trainer: Major P.V. Cazalet

1972			
25th September	Fontwell	Billinghurst Novices' Hurdle	David Mould

COLONIUS
ChG. 1969 Colonist II - Queen of The Isle
Trainer: Major P.V. Cazalet

1972			
24th November	Newbury	Freshman's Novices' Hurdle (Div. II)	David Mould

Trainer: F Walwyn

1974			
21st September	Warwick	Brandon Novices' Chase	Bill Smith

1975			
10th May	Worcester	Bewdley Novices' Chase	Aly Branford
16th May	Startford	Tysoe Novices' Chase (Div. II)	Aly Branford
27th August	Fontwell	Stane Street Chase	Aly Branford
20th October	Fontwell	Barnham Handicap Chase	Aly Branford

1976			
17th April	Towcester	Pomfret Handicap Chase	Bill Smith
10th May	Worcester	Hanbury Handicap Chase	Bill Smith
19th May	Ludlow	Stanton Lacey Handicap Chase	Bill Smith
7th August	Worcester	Tredegar Handicap Chase	Bill Smith
9th August	Worcester	Pomp And Circumstance Chase	Bill Smith
3rd September	Devon and Exeter	Viscountess Petersham Trophy Handicap Chase	Bill Smith
20th September	Plumpton	South Downs Handicap Chase	Bill Smith

1977			
24th August	Fontwell	Bignor Handicap Chase	Bill Smith

COLONELLO
B.G. 1968 Colonist II - Mandella
Trainer: Major P.V. Cazalet

1973
10th January	Plumpton	Heathfield Novices' Hurdle (Div. I)	Bill Smith

Trainer: J. O' Donoghue

1974
26th March	Sandown	Novices' Chase	Charlie Goldsworthy

EARL'S CASTLE
B.G. 1969 Rubor - Castle Inn
Trainer: K. Oliver

1973
13th October	Ayr	Blair Novices' Hurdle (Div. II)	Ron Barry

1974
29th April	Hexham	Dipton Mill Novices' Chase	Ron Barry
20th November	Sedgefield	Chilton Handicap Chase	Colin Tinkler

ISLE OF MAN
B.G. 1967 Manicou - Queen of The Isle
Trainer: F. Walwyn

1973
26th December	Kempton	Yule Tide Hurdle	Terry Biddlecombe

1974
4th January	Sandown	Metropolitan Novices' Hurdle (Div. II Part 1)	Terry Biddlecombe
1st February	Sandown	February Novices' Hurdle (Div. II)	Terry Biddlecombe
1st November	Sandown	November Novices' Chase	Terry Biddlecombe
15th November	Ascot	Hurst Park Novices' Chase	Bill Smith
23rd November	Newbury	Hopeful Chase	Bill Smith

1976
25th February	Windsor	Magna Carta Handicap Chase	Bill Smith
29th October	Sandown	Pirbright Handicap Chase	Bill Smith
6th November	Windsor	Buckinghamshire Handicap Chase	Bill Smith

1977
12th February	Newbury	Newbury Spring Chase	Bill Smith
15th March	Cheltenham	3rd, TWO MILE CHAMPION CHASE	Bill Smith
26th October	Ascot	"Dunkirk" Handicap Chase	Bill Smith

1979
7th March	Worcester	Sidbury Handicap Chase	Bill Smith
16th April	Chepstow	Beachley Handicap Chase	Bill Smith

1980
20th February   Windsor   Magna Carta Handicap Chase   Bill Smith

TAMMUZ
B.G. 1968 Tamerlane - Highlight
Trainer: F. Walwyn

1974
4th January   Sandown   Metropolitan Novices' Hurdle   Bill Smith
                                      (Div. I Part I)
26th December   Kempton   Boxing Day Handicap Hurdle   Bill Smith

1975
16th January   Wincanton   Jamboree Handicap Hurdle   Bill Smith
8th February   Newbury   SCHWEPPES GOLD TROPHY   Bill Smith
                                      HANDICAP HURDLE

COLMAN
Ch.G. 1971 Colonist II - Mandella
Trainer: F. Walwyn

1974
5th October   Towcester   Pattishall Hurdle (Div. II)   Bill Smith

PRESENT ARMS
Ch.G. 1969 Relko - Amicable
Trainer: F. Walwyn

1974
1st November   Sandown   Waterloo Novices' Hurdle (Div. II)   Aly Branford

SUNYBOY
B.H. 1970 Mourne - Fair Bid
Trainer: F. Walwyn

1974
15th November   Ascot   Bingley Novices' Hurdle (Div. II)   Bill Smith
25th November   Wolverhampton Reynoldstown Pattern Hurdle   Bill Smith

1975
1st April   Chepstow   Raglan Novices' Hurdle   Bill Smith
10th April   Ascot   Sardan Novices' Hurdle   Bill Smith

1976

18th February	Ascot	FERNBANK HURDLE	Bill Smith

JUST LIT
Br.G. Eborneezer - Hill Flame
Trainer: F. Walwyn

1974
17th December	Warwick	Shirley Novices' Chase	Bill Smith

BURNING BUSH
B.G. 1970 Lower Boy - Wishbone II
Trainer: K. Oliver

1975
3rd December	Ayr	Lagg Novices' Hurdle (Div. II)	Colin Tinkler

QUEEN'S COLLEGE
B.G. 1971 College Green - Queen of The Isle
Trainer: F Walwyn

1977
12th April	Chepstow	Raglan Novices' Hurdle (Div. I)	Bill Smith

1978
3rd March	Newbury	Burford Novices' Chase (Div. I)	Bill Smith

DESERT WIND
B. G. 1972 Dear Gazelle - Ballyrory
Trainer: F. Walwyn

1977
31st October	Lingfield	Tower Maiden Chase (Div. I)	Bill Smith

1978
3rd March	Newbury	Snelsmore Handicap Chase	Bill Smith
13th May	Hereford	Hereford Novices' Handicap Chase	Bill Smith

SPECIAL CARGO
B. G. 1973 Dairialatan - Little Tot
Trainer: F Walwyn

1979
2nd February	Sandown	February Novices' Hurdle (Div. I)	Bill Smith
21st March	Kempton	Crocus Novices' Hurdle (Div. I)	Bill Smith

4th April	Ascot	Hen Harrier Novices' Hurdle (Div. I)	Bill Smith
1980 26th December	Kempton	Port Wine Novices' Chase	Bill Smith
1981 17th February 31st March	Newton Abbot Sandown	Rippon Tor Novices' Chase Alanbroke Memorial Handicap Chase	Bill Smith Bill Smith
1984 9th March	Sandown	HORSE AND HOUND GRAND MILITARY GOLD CUP CHASE	Mr Gerald Oxley
17th March 27th March 28th April	Lingfield Sandown Sandown	St Patrick's Day Handicap Chase Alanbroke Memorial Handicap Chase WHITBREAD GOLD CUP HANDICAP CHASE	Bill Smith Bill Smith Kevin Mooney
1985 8th March	Sandown	HORSE AND HOUND GRAND MILITARY GOLD CUP CHASE	Mr Gerald Oxley
1986 8th March	Sandown	HORSE AND HOUND GRAND MILITARY GOLD CUP CHASE	Mr Gerald Oxley

UPTON GREY
Gr.G 1974 Rugatino - Colonia
Trainer: F. Walwyn

1978 25th November	Newbury	Wood Speen Novices' Hurdle (Div. II)	Bill Smith
1979 12th May	Hereford	Monmouth Novices' Hurdle (Div. II)	Bill Smith

RHYME ROYAL
Ch. G. 1975 Crepello - Lyrical
Trainer: F. Walwyn

1979 26th December	Kempton	G. J. Novices' Hurdle	Bill Smith

CRANBOURNE TOWER
B. G. 1976 Royal Palace - Heathfield
Trainer: F. Walwyn

1980
| 26th January | Windsor | Rays Novices' Hurdle (Div. I) | Kevin Mooney |
| 24th November | Windsor | White Hart Handicap Hurdle | Kevin Mooney |

1982
| 1st September | Worcester | Alcester Novices' Chase | Bill Smith |

RUSSHILL
Gr.G. 1976 Caliban - Rue Talma
Trainer: F.Walwyn

1980
| 18th December | Startford | Avon Novices' Hurdle (Div. I) | Bill Smith |

1982
| 13th May | Ludlow | Buttercross Novices' Chase | Ricky Pusey |

MASTER ANDREW
B.G. 1975 Hopeful Venture - Conch
Trainer: F.Walwyn

1981
| 3rd December | Warwick | Askett Novices' Hurdle | Bill Smith |

1982
7th January	Lingfield	Horley Novices' Hurdle (Div. II)	Bill Smith
7th April	Ascot	Hen Harrier Novices' Hurdle	Bill Smith
29th December	Warwick	Jacob Marley Novices' Chase	Bill Smith

SINDEBELE
B.G. 1976 War Hawk - West Loch
Trainer: F.Walwyn

1982
| 30th January | Cheltenham | Winchcombe Novices' Hurdle (Div. I) | Stuart Shilston |

SUN RISING
B.G. 1978 Sunyboy - Kipping Hill
Trainer: F. Walwyn

1983
| 25th February | Kempton | Ashford Novices' Hurdle (Div. II) | Bill Smith |

The Winners

1984
18th February   Windsor   Holyport Novices' Handicap Chase   Bill Smith

1987
28th October   Ascot   Bagshot Handicap Chase   Kevin Mooney
12th November   Wincanton   Badger Beer Handicap Chase   Kevin Mooney
21st November   Ascot   The Rip Handicap Chase   Kevin Mooney
28th December   Kempton   Odeon Cinemas Christmas Handicap Chase   Kevin Mooney

LUNEDALE
B.G. 1978 Apollo Eight - Singing Hinny
Trainer: F. Walwyn

1983
3rd September   Stratford   Lady Godiva Novices' Hurdle   Kevin Mooney
22nd October   Startford   Edgehill Novices' Hurdle

1984
3rd November   Stratford   Littleworth Novices' Chase   Kevin Mooney

1985
9th November   Windsor   Saxon House Handicap Chase   Kevin Mooney

1988
12th March   Sandown   Food Brokers Royal Game Handicap Chase   Kevin Mooney

SUNYONE
B.M. 1978 Sunyboy - Wineberry
Trainer: F. Walwyn

1983
12th December   Huntingdon   Haig Whisky Novices' Hurdle   Bill Smith

THE ARGONAUT
Br.G. 1978 Showoff or Captain Jason - Syalbi
Trainer: F. Walwyn

1985
23rd April   Towcester   Abthorpe Novices' Hurdle (Div. I)   Stuart Shilston
6th May   Towcester   Invercote Novices' Handicap Hurdle   Stuart Shilston
24th August   Hereford   Abergavenny Handicap Hurdle   Stuart Shilston
16th November   Warwick   Bonusprint Novices' Chase   Stuart Shilston
14th December   Towcester   Mistletoe Novices' Chase (Div. II)   Stuart Shilston

1986
8th March   Sandown   Dick McCreery Cup Handicap Chase   Mr Mark Bradstock

1987

14th March	Sandown	Dick McCreery Cup Handicap Chase	Mr Mark Bradstock
31st March	Sandown	Downs Handicap Chase	Mr Mark Bradstock
21st October	Cheltenham	Dermot Daly Memorial Trophy Handicap Chase	Mr Gerald Oxley
31st December	Cheltenham	Cleeve Hill Handicap Chase	Stuart Shilston

1988

15th April	Warwick	Bear Handicap Chase	Stuart Shilston

1990

9th March	Sandown	Horse and Hound Grand Military Gold Cup Chase	Mr Gerald Oxley
28th May	Fakenham	Prince of Wales' Cup Chase	Mr Gerald Oxley

Trainer: Mrs F.Walwyn

1991

26th March	Sandown	RMC Group "Ubique" Hunters Chase	Mr Gerald Oxley
27th May	Fakenham	Prince of Wales Cup Chase	Mr Gerald Oxley

YES MASTER
B. or Br.G. 1978 Master Buck - Phayre Vulgan
Trainer: F.Walwyn

1986

10th January	Ascot	Hairy Mary Handicap Hurdle	Kevin Mooney

INSULAR
B.G. 1980 Moulton - Pas de Deux
Trainer: I A Balding

1985

13th November	Newbury	Wood Speen Novices' Hurdle (Div. I)	Brian Reilly

1986

8th March	Sandown	WILLIAM HILL IMPERIAL CUP HANDICAP HURDLE	Eamonn Murphy

1988

21st September	Devon Exeter	Business South West Novices Chase	Peter Scudamore

FIRST ROMANCE
Br. M. 1982 Royalty - Roman Meeting
Trainer: F. Walwyn

1987

20th April	Towcester	Duncote Hurdle (Div. II)	Robert Chapman

DUDLEY
Ch.G. 1983   Owen Dudley - Altruist
Trainer: F. Walwyn

1990			
22nd February	Folkestone	EBF Novices Hurdle	Kevin Mooney

ADMIRAL'S LEAP
Ch.G. 1984   Quayside - Sailor's Will
Trainer: F. Walwyn

1990			
22nd February	Folkestone	Gerald Glover Stayers' Novice Hurdle	Kevin Mooney
1991			
13th April	Southwell	Rolleston Mill Novices' Chase	Kevin Mooney

ROYAL PAVILION
Ch.G. 1983   Royalty - Manushi
Trainer: Mrs F. Walwyn

1990			
3rd November	Sandown	Total Heating Novices' Chase	Kevin Mooney

FURRY KNOWE
B.G. 1985   Furry Glen - I Know
Trainer: Mrs F. Walwyn

1990			
7th November	Newbury	Wood Speen Novices' Hurdle (Div. I)	Kevin Mooney
1991			
6th May	Devon and Exeter	Portman Building Society Novices' Hurdle	Kevin Mooney
1992			
1st January	Devon and Exeter	David Garrett Memorial Challenge Trophy Novices' Chase	Ben De Haan

DALLISTON
Br.G. 1986   March Legend - Auklyn
Trainer: Mrs F. Walwyn

1992			
18th April	Southwell	Thurgaton Novices' Handicap Hurdle	Ben De Haan

NORMAN CONQUEROR
Br.G. 1985 Royal Fountain - Constant Rose
Trainer: T. Thomson Jones

1992			
20th November	Ascot	Punch Bowl Handicap Chase	Mr Stephen Swiers

LUNABELLE
B.M. 1988 Idiot's Delight - Barbella
Trainer: I A Balding

1992			
26th December	Wincanton	Pleasure Prints Photographers Novices' Hurdle	Jimmy Frost
1993			
27th September	Fontwell	Bunnahabhain Novices' Chase	Jimmy Frost

SKINNHILL
B.G. 1984 Final Straw - Twenty Two
Trainer: T. Thomson Jones

1993			
13th March	Wolverhampton	Horse Guards Parade Handicap Chase	Steve Smith Eccles

KEEL ROW
B.F. 1990 Relkino - Caserta
Trainer: T Thomson Jones

1995			
16th January	Fontwell	EBF National Hunt Flat Race	Mick Fitzgerald

BASS ROCK
B.G. 1988 Bellypha - Dunfermline
Trainer: I A Balding

1994			
23rd March	Exeter	EBF National Hunt Novices' Hurdle	Jimmy Frost
12th October	Exeter	Dean and Dyball Handicap Hurdle	Jamie Osborne

MOAT GARDEN
B.G.   1988   Sportin' Life - Round Tower
Trainer: I A Balding

1993
20th November	Market Rasen	Clugston Novices' Hurdle	Jimmy Frost
30th December	Taunton	Holly Tree Novices' Hurdle	Jimmy Frost

WHITECHAPEL
B.G. 1988   Arctic Tern - Christchurch
Trainer: N. J. Henderson

1994
19th March	Chepstow	Beagles Novices' Hurdle	Mick Fitzgerald

NEARCO BAY
B.G. Double Nearco - Ahi Ua
Trainer: N. J. Henderson

1994
4th April	Hereford	Newton Williams Handicap Chase	John Kavanagh
30th April	Hereford	Knight Frank and Rutley Handicap Chase	John Kavanagh
11th May	Hereford	Canon Pyon Handicap Chase	John Kavanagh
30th May	Uttoxeter	Neville Lumb Silver Jubilee Handicap Chase	John Kavanagh
12th October	Uttoxeter	Trent Bathrooms Handicap Chase	John Kavanagh

BRAES OF MAR
B.G.   Bustino - Barbello
Trainer: N. J. Henderson

1994
2nd December	Sandown	E.B.F. NH Novices' Hurdle (Qualifier)	John Kavanagh

Index

Index

Index

Index

Other books published by
Pride of Place (UK) Ltd

Racing

Laurel Queen's Claim to Fame by Andrew Hoyle
Hbk ISBN No 1874645140   £14.99

After winning 22 races Laurel Queen is the most prolific winning mare ever recorded. This book is the story of the blood, sweat and tears that have gone into the making of such a successful horse. If anyone wants to see what goes on behind the scenes of racehorse training then this book is a must.

From Rags to Riches by John Budden
Pbk ISBN No 187464506X   £7.99

Everyone wants a bargain, everyone loves a champion. This book is the story of 16 horses that have been both, including Gold Cup winner Jodami, champion Hurdler Flaky Dove, the nation's favourite filly Lochsong, classic winners Bob Return and Mister Baileys, etc.

Betting

The Golf Form Book 1995 by Keith Elliott
pbk ISBN No 1874645205   £14.99, Hbk ISBN No 1874645086   £19.99

Golf betting is growing faster than any other form of betting. This book gives player profiles of over 200 International players and all the results of golf tournaments in 1994. A definite asset for any golf enthusiast or gambler and a welcome companion for armchair tournament devotee's.

> In that age old war with our greatest enemy the bookmaker, this book is a deadly weapon - an invaluable guide to successful golf betting.
> review by Derek Mcgovern, Sports Editor, The Racing Post

Always Back Winners by Stuart Simpson
pbk ISBN No 1874645043   £9.99

Reprinted for the 3rd time within 9 months. A book with a cult following.

> This book has already sold out once so don't miss out on what is probably the most sought after racing system ever published.
> review by Nick Mordin, Sporting Life.

For more information on our forthcoming titles **telephone: 01257-246005**